Hypnotherapy for Happiness: Easing Anxiety

Alexandra Hopkins

BALBOA.
PRESS
A DIVISION OF HAY HOUSE

Balboa Press books may be ordered through booksellers or by contacting:

Balboa Press
A Division of Hay House
1663 Liberty Drive
Bloomington, IN 47403
www.balboapress.com
1-(877) 407-4847

Because of the dynamic nature of the Internet, any web addresses or links contained in this book may have changed since publication and may no longer be valid. The views expressed in this work are solely those of the author and do not necessarily reflect the views of the publisher, and the publisher hereby disclaims any responsibility for them.

The author of this book does not dispense medical advice or prescribe the use of any technique as a form of treatment for physical, emotional, or medical problems without the advice of a physician, either directly or indirectly. The intent of the author is only to offer information of a general nature to help you in your quest for emotional and spiritual well-being. In the event you use any of the information in this book for yourself, which is your constitutional right, the author and the publisher assume no responsibility for your actions.

Any people depicted in stock imagery provided by Thinkstock are models, and such images are being used for illustrative purposes only.
Certain stock imagery © Thinkstock.

Printed in the United States of America

ISBN: 978-1-4525-7009-9 (sc)
ISBN: 978-1-4525-7010-5 (e)

Balboa Press rev. date: 03/14/2013

DISCLAIMER

I am not a psychologist, and as I type, I am not yet a counsellor, (although I am currently undertaking a counselling diploma), so I don't consider myself to be an academic authority on the mechanics of the workings of the mind.

I would like to stress, that this book is purely observational and based on MY experiences of working with hundreds of clients. Psychologists and counsellors may well disagree with my observations, but I feel that the information in this book is just as relevant as it is reflecting the reality of the accumulation of my clients thoughts, feelings, behaviours, beliefs and issues.

Additionally, I don't claim to speak for all hypnotherapists. Most hypnotherapists have their own preferences and work in their own unique way. I consider this book to reflect MY experience.

All examples used in the book are non-specific to any one client . . . they are more collective or generic, because even though some seem quite particular, they are included because they've occurred multiple times over several clients or I have compiled one example from several different case studies to illustrate a point. Any similarity to any one client is purely coincidental.

I would like to advise anyone thinking of visiting a hypnotherapist to check their credentials, specifically to see whether they are a member of their country or state's professional hypnotherapists' association/s. These associations regulate the industry to make hypnotherapists accountable by maintaining continuing professional development and operating all within a Code of Ethics. Obtaining this information before booking your appointment will help give you peace of mind that you are in good hands.

TABLE OF CONTENTS

DEDICATION

Through my work as a Hypnotherapist, I have learnt something valuable. That every person that we encounter, and every experience that we have with people, contributes to where we are standing right now . . . Therefore, this book is dedicated to all those people who I have encountered in my life, who have brought me to this point in time and contributed to who I am today . . . and I am proud to be that person . . .

My family and friends throughout my ages, including those who have come and gone. There are those who have encouraged, supported and believed in me. There are also those who have caused pain, challenged and exasperated me . . . But regardless of whether the lesson presented to me has been easy or hard, I have gained something precious from each and every one of you.

To every client that has allowed me into their lives for just a brief time . . . I feel honoured that you have done so. I appreciate that you have shared your turmoil with me, however hard that might have been. My hope is that through our experiences together—that has culminated in the writing of this book—others may be inspired to take their first step toward their own happiness too.

ACKNOWLEDGEMENT PAGE

Having never written or published a book before, means that the process of actually producing this book has been a challenge. I would like to thank those who have helped make it a physical reality. I have come to appreciate the value of my wonderful editor, Elizabeth Bezant—writing coach, whose pencil marks scrawled all over my manuscript—I have had a love-hate relationship with!

To Heidi R—photographer, who has probably taken the only photo of me that I've actually ever liked! Thank you for capturing my image in a way that I am proud to show to the world.

To Sally Evans—graphic designer, who sat with me for hours trying to interpret that which has been in my head for the book cover . . . whilst simultaneously cooking dinner, feeding the dog and tending to the children! Thank you for finding the time to help make my vision a reality.

To my dear friend Tania Townsend, a fellow hypnotherapist, who cast her eye over my words to ensure that what I said was true to our profession, and who has also encouraged me every step of the way, with her complete belief in me. I thank you so much for your love and support.

To Jennifer Wilson, colleague and psychologist, but primarily, dear friend. She has written the 'afterword' to this book and has endorsed it from her professional viewpoint. I have always valued and respected her opinion, and so her support of my book, has meant so much.

To another dear friend, Danielle Schwarzer, who unselfishly read my manuscript at my request, so that I could determine whether I had got my message across, or would just confuse everybody! Thankfully, I was encouraged by her words . . . especially as I have come to greatly value her opinions and support over the many years that we have known each other.

*Thank you to you all, as you have all
helped me achieve my dream.*

FOREWORD

We all have automatic responses to specific situations whether we realise it or not. Whether it be a fear of flying, the need to eat when nervous, an unexplained anger in certain situations, or something totally different, we all have our own idiosyncrasies and I for one thought mine, annoying as they are, were here to stay. Turns out I was wrong.

In her book, Hypnotherapy for Happiness: Easing Anxiety, Alexandra not only demystifies hypnotherapy and offers insights in to why we react the way we do, but she also offers us hope by explaining in everyday language how hypnosis can help us change our reactions. This is no text book that you have to wade through to find an answer. It's filled with case studies and examples explained in everyday language, and after reading this book everybody will understand the possibilities offered by hypnotherapy.

With all of this knowledge came that wonderful realisation that I don't react the way I do because I'm crazy, but because something minor happened to me when I was younger and now my mind simply wants to protect me from it happening again.

Elizabeth Bezant
Writing Coach
www.writingtoinspire.com

'What the mind can conceive, it can achieve'.

Napolean Hill

INTRODUCTION

WHY AM I WRITING THIS BOOK?

I've been thinking about writing this book for quite some time now. Writing a book, for me, is about sharing information with other people in the hope that it might help them in some way—it might give them new information which could lead to a better understanding of themselves, who they are, why they do what they do and how they might find answers and solutions to their problems. This book though, more specifically, has been written to help people understand their anxiety and why it even exists, and then show them that they don't have to put up with it—*there is a solution.*

I am a hypnotherapist, and as such, people have let me into their lives to witness their turmoil, and to help them overcome their anxiety. It's the most rewarding thing I have ever experienced . . . to actually be instrumental in a person finding their inner peace and happiness.

*Anxiety comes in all sorts of shapes and sizes
and flavours—from general everyday worry
and stress to utterly debilitating fears and
phobias . . . and everything in-between.*

*It's your subconscious' response to something it
doesn't like—based on its first experience with
the underlying emotion—and on feeling that
emotion again, it enacts its job as 'protector' to
either stay and fight, avoid or run like hell!*

*How do you cope with your anxiety? Do you smoke 40
cigarettes a day, eat the entire contents of your fridge every
night, avoid situations that make you feel nervous or do
you simply avoid, suppress, numb or side-step around
your emotions to make sure you don't wake them up?*

It's apparent to me that everyone carries some level of anxiety within them, and that this level fluctuates during a lifetime, depending on the things that are happening around them and to them. These happenings trigger an emotion and it's these emotions that *without exception* are at the heart of *all* anxiety (even for those of you who think you are 'emotionless'). When I help clients understand which emotions are involved, and how and why they are being triggered, the sense of relief the client feels just to have a reason for all their angst is, in itself, therapeutic . . . because not understanding the 'why' together with experiencing the feeling of being completely out of all control, can also add to the anxiety.

*Through this book, I hope to help people start
to make sense of their own unique anxiety, so
they can finally understand why it's really there,
thereby taking the first step to overcoming it.*

Helping people in the way that I do, has woken me up to the enormity of the *'anxiety crisis'* in our world today. I don't know if it's always been at such a high level, but I do know that it affects a massive percentage of our population. It affects all age-groups—from young children to the classic 'mid-life crisis' 35-50 age group and it seems to me, quite alarmingly, that anxiety amongst our teenagers and young adults is spiralling out of control.

So what can be done about it? Do people have to put up with it and resign themselves to a life-long struggle? Do they have to continually try to hide it from the world? (It amazes me how many people don't tell anyone about their inner turmoil for fear of judgement, ridicule or embarrassment.) The answer to this question, you'll be pleased to hear, is NO! There is a solution—an effective, relatively painless, and quick one . . . and that solution is . . .

Hypnotherapy!

The very reason I have actually stepped completely out of my comfort-zone and challenged all of my own insecurities and short-comings to even think about writing a book, is because the urge to share this **amazing solution to anxiety** is far greater than my fear of setting myself such a daunting challenge. I'm *bursting* to share the wonder of hypnotherapy through my own experience as a hypnotherapist. I get truly overwhelmed seeing this amazing therapy work time and time again. When I've just witnessed a client make the most wonderful breakthrough in their life—I literally want to run outside, stop people in the street and say, 'Did you know this lady has just overcome her life-long battle with panic attacks by using hypnotherapy?—It can help you too, and you, and you . . .'

As you read through this book, you'll notice how the same things seem to come up again and again. However, I've repeated myself intentionally so, as the reader, you can see how the same type of event can cause different issues, or how the same issues can be caused by completely different events. Why? Because even though we can generalise a person's issue by putting it into a category and stamping a label on it, ultimately, each person's anxiety is completely unique to them.

The effectiveness of hypnotherapy certainly amazes me each and every day as I watch my clients go through profound life changes. At the ripe old age of 43, I can't believe that I've gotten through most of my life not really knowing that hypnotherapy even existed. Not that I'm the only one—I'm finding that when people discover I'm a hypnotherapist, their reactions are anything from giving me a vacant look to giving me that 'you must be a nutcase then' look, as they back away slowly and run for the hills. Ultimately, I know that's because most people have absolutely no understanding of what hypnotherapy *actually* is or how it can help people.

Well, when I say that I didn't know, and most people don't know it exists, that's not quite true. I, like many people, have watched the stage-hypnotists on television, and laughed uncontrollably whilst watching people clucking like chickens and serenading broomsticks in front of hundreds of people. I was also aware that some people would go to a hypnotherapist to give up smoking, but that was the extent of my knowledge. In fact, I believe it is still what most people think when the word hypnotherapy is mentioned—the power of television!

'So what else is there?' I hear you ask. Well answering that question is *exactly* why I'm writing this book—because there's *so much more,* and as such, I've decided to make it my mission to . . .

De-mystify Hypnotherapy

I want to introduce it into *your* life as an easily accessible, wonderfully versatile and relatively fast-working therapy that I hope will become one of the mainstream options available to anyone looking to make changes in their life. So, for your information, and also to justify any possible misconceptions, I'm not strange, I don't dress in rainbow-coloured dresses with flowers in my hair, and I don't see my clients in a dimly-lit incense smoke-filled back room of my house—*no!*

I'm from a business-background having helped my ex-husband run a commercial interior design business for over 16 years. I consider myself to be a very logical, practical and level-headed person. I run my hypnotherapy business from a professionally presented suite of offices in Western Australia. I am accepted as a credible member of a business networking group where I've already started to awaken my fellow 'networkers' to the reality of what I do, rather than the myth. In fact it's great to see their awareness changing as they realise that what I do is a credible and effective form of helping people change their lives.

Because they, like most people, would assume that anyone looking to make changes, or to cope with stress and anxiety, or to overcome fears and phobias, would accept that going to see a counsellor or a psychologist was probably their best, and possibly, only option . . . or at least the only option they would admit to trying! It's true I've had many a client who has come to see me and not told anyone that they are receiving hypnotherapy for fear of ridicule from their friends or family.

So, as such, I'm hoping this book will do its job and remove fear, correct any misinformation surrounding hypnotherapy, and hopefully light a spark of interest. If I do a *really* good job, it might even ignite a sense of excitement within you as I share examples of how and why it works. Through re-telling stories of 'actual' change I could in turn awaken . . .

The potential that exists within YOU to make YOUR own changes using hypnotherapy

Imagine living a life having eased your fears, anxieties and phobias, your feelings of not being good enough or changing any unwanted habits . . . or in fact, changing any thought that is holding you back. Interested? Then read on—this book will give you hope that there is the possibility that this could become YOUR reality!

PART 1

WHO ARE YOU AND WHY DO YOU HAVE ANXIETY?

CHAPTER 1

WHO ARE YOU?

Firstly, let's establish who you are and the basics of why you're the way you are. This is vital information EVERY person should know. In fact I would like to see children being taught this stuff in school—I absolutely believe it would prevent an awful lot of unnecessary turmoil if students, indeed everyone, had a basic understanding of the way their mind works.

With an understanding of how your mind works, you will then also understand how and why hypnotherapy works.

The Conscious and Subconscious Minds

First of all, your mind is split into two, and the split is definitely <u>not</u> fifty/fifty. The conscious mind is the small part, containing all your logic, reasoning, short term memory and will-power. It exists very much in the 'here and now', it's also the part that can drift off, get distracted and fall asleep, etc, etc . . .

Then you have the HUGE and powerful **subconscious mind**, where pretty much everything else lives—your belief systems, automatic responses, long-term memory, including the memories of ALL your life's experiences and it's also where your emotions are triggered from. The subconscious mind never falls asleep and never forgets anything. It records *everything* you experience, almost like a video recorder . . . whoops showing my age there . . . let's make that a high-tech DVD recorder with super multi-format recording with 1080p up-scaling capabilities (hopefully I've not lost the younger readers now I've put that in ☺).

Now, these 'recorded' life experiences of yours help to create your **'belief systems'.** These are the beliefs that you hold about how the world works, where your place within the world is, and how best to survive in it, and ultimately . . .

> *The subconscious mind acts primarily, out*
> *of the need to protect you and everything it*
> *does is triggered by emotion—not logic!*

In other words, it looks out for you and makes sure you get through life as safely as possible, also getting you through life by doing most things on auto-pilot.

Auto-Pilot

'Auto-pilot—what's that about?' I hear you ask. Well, your physical body is regulated using auto-pilot, so that all the systems of your body will continue to operate without you having to consciously be mindful of carrying out each and every function. It's also where the subconscious mind, through your early life's experiences, learns how to respond to stimuli and events that spark off an emotion. It remembers your original response, then that first response becomes

the automatic reaction, carried out every time the subconscious mind experiences the same emotion in the future.

Auto-pilot can be both a help and a hindrance. If you didn't go through most of your life on auto-pilot, it would be a nightmare! You'd have to consciously think about every little thing you did during your day. You'd have to think about taking each breath, how to put one foot in front of the other, or even how to respond when someone said 'Hello' to you. Could you imagine getting in your car each day and thinking about every movement you'd have to make just to drive your car to work?—like I said it would be a *nightmare!*

So, considering auto-pilot helps you in many different ways to get through your life with relative ease . . . why then can it *also* be a hindrance? Because included in your selection of automatic behaviours that are locked in, are all your *unwanted* emotional responses to things that happen during your day. For example:

You're driving on the freeway, when someone pulls out in front of you, and before you know it, you feel that uncontrollable anger rising in your chest. Then, before you ask yourself, 'do I really want to wind down the window and shout out at the top of my voice, 'you **@@!!' the window is down, and out comes a tirade of expletives that you realise, as you catch the startled look on your children's faces in the rear view mirror, were <u>extremely</u> inappropriate. You feel mortified and guilty, and can't believe you would behave so badly. You ask yourself, 'Why on earth do I always do that?'

You end up having a little battle in your head and berate yourself, tell yourself you won't do it next time, like all the other times before, and apologise to the kids (and make them promise they won't tell anyone). But despite all your good intentions, the next time it happens all over again. <u>What's that all about?</u>

Well, you can thank auto-pilot for that too! That's my point . . . the good *and* the bad are all on auto-pilot, and whilst we don't want to change the good stuff, we certainly would *love* to change the bad stuff—but how? Because you've tried again, and again, and again, and still nothing changes.

Hypnotherapy can help!

***Why keep putting up with those things
you don't want to do anymore?***

Go and see a hypnotherapist near you!

But, anyway . . . I'm getting carried away again . . . back to you! So the big question really is, why is it that you behave like a raving banshee when someone cuts you up on the road, and yet find yourself enviously watching your spouse's cool-as-a-cucumber response to the same life-threatening perils on the freeway? *How does he do that?* In fact, his serene actions just make you feel even worse about yourself. Then your mind gets carried away and you assume there's something terribly wrong with you and you start to beat yourself up about it, and before you know it, it's become a huge issue in your life that you just want gone!

The reason that you act the way you do, in any situation, is the result of how you learnt to respond to certain situations when you were growing up.

***You are a unique human being . . . what makes you unique
is that the sum of your life experiences is like no-one
else's. <u>Nobody</u> has experienced everything that you have.***

As we grow up and have an experience that triggers an emotion that we haven't felt before, the subconscious decides on the best way to react and records this initial response if it feels it was effective. For example:

When you were three years old, your father shouted at you when he came home drunk from the pub one evening and this scared you. The subconscious decided that the best course of action to keep you safe, was to run away from him and to stay in your bedroom. From that point onwards, whenever he was drunk or even shouted at you, you immediately retreated to your room to avoid the potential 'danger'. Now, as an adult, you bring that same automatic response into your day-to-day life. You find yourself getting quite anxious whenever you encounter <u>any</u> form of confrontation as you feel your body getting ready to run!

The subconscious likes an easy life and as you can see from the above example, once it has a response that seemed to work the first time, whenever it experiences a similar situation on the same emotional level in the future, it simply responds in the same way. This response then becomes an **'automatic subconscious pattern of behaviour'** that is enacted with little or no conscious input—no wonder change is so difficult!

And we don't just have the one automatic response, we have loads! We have a different one for *each* emotion that we experience . . . and all of our emotions are being continually triggered by events in our daily lives. In fact, we are a walking collection of automatic responses—and we use them to get through every day on auto pilot.

Now, as you were reading that previous bit, it might have occurred to you that most of your automatic responses were created in childhood. After all, I did mention that the subconscious bases its automatic responses on what happened the '*first time*' it encountered a certain kind of situation . . . and you'd be right, pretty much.

Since the creation of your automatic responses in childhood, not much has changed.

However, subsequent events could magnify those responses and that's why some issues may *appear* to start later in life. Yet in reality they are actually a re-sensitisation of a past initiation.

Belief Systems

The subconscious is very pre-occupied with enacting all of your automatic responses, but this isn't it's only focus. Also in the mix, as I mentioned earlier . . .

> ***You hold your belief systems in the subconscious mind and it's the subconscious' job to sustain those belief systems.***

This makes the subconscious feel safe, because it's what it knows. It doesn't much care if it appears to be positive or negative to you consciously and logically, it just knows it has to match it. For example, you might have grown up in a household with a father who would often say, 'You're useless, you can't do anything right!' You then adopt a belief system that says, 'I'm a failure'.

Now, let's take this 'I'm a failure' belief system as an example and I'll briefly explain how it can have a profound effect on your life . . .

> *You grow up assuming that this is indeed the case—*
> *'I am a failure!' It might not be something you're mindfully*
> *aware of, but if you did stop and check out your 'self-talk'*
> *you'd probably find yourself constantly saying things like,*
> *'I can't do that', or 'I'm not very good at this'.*
> (That's if you stop and listen. Most of us are saying things
> to ourselves every moment of the day, but of course
> we don't really acknowledge what it is we're saying).

Now, as you grow up, you start to expand your awareness and you realise that people out in the big wide world are actually being successes at all sorts of things and you consciously think to yourself, 'Hmmm, I'd really like to be a success too. I'd like to go to University and study a business degree and run my own business—I like the sound of that!'

So you take steps to put these plans in place. You're all excited about the future, but half-way through your course, you find that you're procrastinating when you should be studying, or it seems much more appealing to hang out with your friends than write essays, and slowly your grades start to slide. Then, before you know it, you're so far behind in your studies that there's no way you'll ever catch up, let alone obtain your degree . . . and, hey presto! . . . you remain the failure that you know yourself to be. Consciously you feel <u>so</u> disappointed in yourself, but subconsciously it's feeling quite good—job done!

This is a prime example of self-sabotage and the subconscious is a master at it. In fact, it is often its tool of choice to keep those belief systems going.

So, here you are, a combination of past experiences, memories, belief systems and automatic behaviours, all of which are pretty much 'set in stone'. What do you do now?

<u>**Hypnotherapy!**</u>

<u>**Why does it work? Because it allows you access to the subconscious mind where ALL your memories, belief systems and automatic behaviours live.**</u>

Everyone Should Know
How Their Own Mind Works

I explain the workings of the mind (as I've done in this book) to ALL my clients before they enter into hypnotherapy. That way they know exactly why they're experiencing the issues they're having. It's amazing to watch their facial expression start to relax as the awareness takes over and they realise they are simply caught up in the cycle of automatic responses and belief systems created by their childhood. People can make a slight positive shift right there, primarily because they have a reason for the frustration they've been experiencing. It can also stop them continually beating themselves up over some of the things they find themselves doing. That's not to say they shouldn't take ownership of them, but more that they can see they've been created by circumstances.

Imagine how different it would be if kids were armed with this awareness because they had been taught it in school, if they had this basic understanding of how their mind works and how it's contributed to all of their automatic responses. They're taught a myriad of things they're not likely to need or want in adult life and yet they're not taught something that would *absolutely* help them in their future lives no matter whether they decided to be a teacher, a dentist, a sales rep, a factory worker, a graphic designer, a stay-at-home mum, etc.

The teenage years are especially challenging trying to cope with new experiences that the big wide world has to offer. However, armed with knowledge of how their mind works, teenagers might be able to cope with this stage of life more positively instead of internalising their negative feelings or beating themselves up (sometimes to the point of losing their self-worth and self-esteem or giving up all hope that things could be different). I also think it would encourage people at any age, to quickly seek help when experiencing symptoms of anxiety, rather than assuming that they're just 'wrong' or 'unfixable' and resigning themselves to putting up with their negative issues throughout their entire lives.

I have an increasing number of teenage clients who sit in my chair, frightened and confused by their anxiety. They don't understand the overwhelming emotion that instils a feeling of 'not being in control' of their mind and body. How different would it be for them if they understood there *was* a reason for what they were doing and how they were feeling and that things *could* be changed and that they *could* take back control?

But, back to the plot! . . .

The reason I've explained how you became the way you are, is because it's the basis of how *I* work as a hypnotherapist. In *my* mind, the way to help people as a hypnotherapist is not just to alleviate the symptoms of what they are experiencing, i.e. anxiety and stress, instead . . .

'I consider it to be <u>vital</u> to firstly find the '<u>cause</u>' of
why they are experiencing the symptoms of their
issue . . . finding the starting point . . . <u>the 'experience'</u>
that set up their automatic response the <u>first time</u>.

I'll explain more on this in another chapter . . . but first, let's talk about the white elephant in the room—hypnosis!

CHAPTER 2

LET'S DE-MYSTIFY HYPNOSIS!

B efore I go further into hypno-*therapy* . . . I feel it's my duty to 'de-mystify' the tool of hypnotherapy, which is *hypnosis*.

Hands up who thinks hypnosis is spooky, scary and just plain freaky!

Hands up who thinks hypnosis is mind-control!

Hands up who thinks you have to be one of those people who dance through rainbows and hug trees to even think about having hypnosis!

I think that's most of you with your hands in the air now! And, as I said earlier, you can probably thank television for that.

The purpose of this book isn't to offer an instruction manual of *how* to hypnotise someone . . . it's to illustrate how the 'state' of hypnosis can be used for therapeutic purposes to effect profound and lasting change, and ultimately to help people overcome their anxiety. Generally, people tend to be scared of hypnosis because they don't understand it, mostly because their *only* experience of it is through television where it's usually portrayed as being a way to make someone look ridiculous—as in stage hypnosis, or as sinister mind control in some dark movie genre.

So, to help introduce it into the real world, I want to explain the hypnotic state of mind in basic terms (because I'm not expecting you to be able to write a thesis on it by the end of the book).

Conscious VS Subconscious

Let's go back to the conscious and subconscious parts of your mind. These two parts, although they can operate independently of each other, are also intertwined. They work together to ensure that the things that are accepted by the subconscious mind are considered logically 'safe' by the conscious part.

Generally, these two parts of the mind work as an effective team, however, they can also contribute to being stuck in negative patterns of behaviour. The over-zealous conscious mind can interfere with the potential to change by considering it to be unlikely, taking into consideration past failed attempts. The subconscious mind has a general resistance toward change, because it feels safe with what it knows and likes an easy life. As a result, it is far more focused on enacting the same responses again, and again, and again . . . all of this means that the idea of positive change is generally not enough to make it become a reality.

This is where hypnosis does a wonderful thing—it encourages the conscious part of the mind to 'step aside' as it were. This means that the conscious mind wanders off from its position as 'gatekeeper' to the subconscious mind, which results in the subconscious suddenly becoming accessible and 'open'. This state of mind where the two parts are separated, is called 'dissociation'.

Dissociation

Dissociation is a natural state of mind, but can also be induced by a hypnotist 'on demand', and methods of induction can vary. The hypnotist can use rapid methods that confuse and overload the conscious mind, or slower, more relaxing methods to help bore the conscious mind into wandering off somewhere else. The conscious mind has a fairly short attention span and if what's happening around it is monotonous enough, it will generally find something more interesting to think about. You might remember a time when you were daydreaming when in fact you should have been listening to what someone was saying.

Once dissociation is achieved, the hypnotist can give positive suggestions to the subconscious, so that it can readily accept them as a new beneficial way of doing things. It also allows the hypnotist access to helpful information that the subconscious is storing in its long term memory. This information can show connections between past events and current issues. Direct access to the subconscious, without interference from the conscious mind, can result in change actually taking place.

However, this is where the fear comes in for many clients . . . 'Oh my God! . . . If you have access to the part of my mind that knows everything, you could get my bank details, or take control of my mind and make me go out and rob a bank!'

Hypnosis Myths

It's a shame that the fear factor surrounding hypnosis overshadows all the amazingly positive things it can achieve—but scare-mongering always seems to spread a lot quicker and easier than good news! When you read further on in the book to the stories inspired by clients' true life experiences of a hypnotic trance, you'll realise that a person's awareness is usually sufficient for them to remember much, if not all, of their experience. Their conscious mind is still present enough to perceive if something is wrong. Ultimately, a person's subconscious is their protector and as such, it wouldn't allow any suggestions in that would go against its primary moral code. *(For added peace of mind, I would also advise anyone thinking of visiting a hypnotherapist to check their credentials).*

What Does It Feel Like To Be Hypnotised?

Most people expect to feel like a zombie during hypnosis, believing they won't remember a thing. I think they assume that when they sit in the chair, that I'm going to 'knock them out' and that they'll wake up at the end, and walk out of the office a completely new person, with absolutely no awareness of what happened.

Therefore, they are usually surprised to feel mostly 'with-it' during the session. I've even had people leave the office completely disappointed that they felt awake—they had actually wanted the complete 'zombie experience'. They had wanted to '*feel*' hypnotised—even though they didn't know what that would feel like—and they leave feeling disappointed because they assume that they weren't, in fact, hypnotised. But when they come back for their next session, they are completely surprised at how they must indeed have been 'under' because of the obvious changes they've experienced.

The truth of the matter is . . . everyone is different, and everyone experiences hypnosis in their own unique way. Some feel alert and focused, while others periodically nod off because they're so relaxed. Most, I would say, feel sort of 'daydreamy'. The most frequent response is that the client can hear most of what I say, but can't always concentrate on what I'm saying, and that their conscious mind quickly drifts off, bored, and they find themselves thinking about what to buy on the way home for tea, or go over what they did yesterday. Then they might catch the odd word that I say, and go into a mild panic thinking 'Oh my God—was I supposed to listen to that? Was I supposed to do something then?' However, the conscious mind soon gets bored again as it realises I'm still droning on and so off it goes again.

During a session, a client won't tend to just stay at any one level, but will 'rotate' between being alert, to feeling a bit 'daydreamy', to nearly nodding off and then 'jumping' as their awareness comes flooding back and then they slowly slide back into daydreaminess, and around they go again.

When I'm hypnotised, I tend to stay quite alert in the mind but I sort of think 'You know, I could open my eyes right now—but I can't be bothered,' or 'I could actually get up and walk out if I wanted to—but I can't *really* be bothered' . . . and that's about the extent of what I 'feel'.

The subconscious often affects the physical body and how it feels during hypnosis. It's common to experience twitchy extremities, especially the fingers. Some people find their skin gets a little 'tingly' and they spend much of the session wanting to scratch the itch. They worry, of course, because they think that if they move they'll 'break the spell' and come out of hypnosis—but I tell clients that those people you see running around the stage and screaming on telly don't seem to have a problem with moving when they are hypnotised—so scratch away!

Their physical body can also feel quite 'heavy', as though they couldn't lift their arm up or move their legs . . . alternatively they can even lose much of the sensation in the body. Some people who come in suffering physical pain, can feel no pain whatsoever during the hypnosis. One of my clients, as I was progressing through her session, started to raise her arms . . . very slowly at first so that just her fingers were off the arms of the chair. Then when I looked again, her hands was hovering above the arm rest, and then her arms started to rise, very slowly, until they were vertically up in the air and she stayed like this for the remainder of the session, which was a full half-hour. I asked her afterwards what was going on with the arms. 'I felt them go up,' she said. 'I didn't really question it, they just seemed to want to and it felt quite comfortable really so I left them there.'

Some people do actually fall asleep and snore and dribble. My son dribbles during hypnosis and then, when he comes out of it, swears he wasn't hypnotised. Remember, it's only the conscious part of your mind that sleeps, the subconscious remains wide awake, so even if you nod off during hypnosis, the subconscious will still be listening to everything I say.

Now, even though you might be thinking that sleeping is the ultimate method to get the conscious mind out of the way, it's not my preferred state for clients. Given a choice, I prefer clients to stay awake. This way, they can have enough awareness, as they listen to my words, to actively direct their thoughts. These thoughts, in turn, evoke emotion that the subconscious would be 'tuned into' and this helps us 'do the work'. **The imagination is the 'language' of the subconscious mind** and, believe it or not . . .

The subconscious doesn't know there's any difference between imagination and reality.

Yes I know! I couldn't believe that either when I first heard it—but it's true! The good thing is, that when you know this, you can actually use it, both in hypnosis and during your day-to-day life, to your advantage. I'll go into that in more detail later in the book.

How Hypnosis Enables Positive Change

During hypnosis, if the hypnotherapist is directing your thoughts to rehearse how it will feel to experience the positive changes you want to make, the subconscious can get carried away thinking what you're imagining is actually happening now. As it tunes into the good feelings that go along with your 'daydreaming' it realises what a great experience it's having, and this spurs it on to adopt it as a preference to the old, negative way of doing things. Therefore a change in behaviour is more likely . . . especially since the conscious mind is out of the way enough, so is not watching and saying to itself *'Yeah . . . like that could ever happen . . . who are you trying to kid?'*

So in a nutshell, that's what hypnosis is, and how it might feel to experience it.

What about hypno-***therapy*** then? Hypnosis gets access into the subconscious mind—the 'therapy' part means that the hypnotist has some tools in their bag to help you, the client, do some positive work whilst they're in there. On that note, you might ask, 'Are all hypnotherapists the same?' The answer is NO! . . . which, I'm sure will inspire another question in you . . . 'How do I find the one who is going to help *me?*'

CHAPTER 3

HOW TO FIND A HYPNOTHERAPIST TO SUIT YOU

I encourage clients to ring around a few other hypnotherapists to see who they 'feel' would be right for them, because indeed, hypnotherapists are not all the same. Through mixing and talking to other hypnotherapists, I know that many of them use various other tools from their 'Tool Bag'. In fact, I think it's rare to come across one who focuses solely on a basic version of hypnotherapy.

For example, I've done research that's helped me to focus on regressing clients and finding the cause of their issues. I'm also undergoing a counselling diploma and I'm continually reading books on hypnotherapy to gain any further information that can help me to help a client. On top of this, the professional development requirements of my membership of the Hypnotherapist Association to which I belong, stipulates that ongoing training is compulsory.

Other hypnotherapists are likely to have *their* own collection of modalities that they are qualified in, whether it be mind-based like psychology or counselling, or physically based, like kinesiology or reflexology. Each hypnotherapist puts it all together in their own unique way, enabling them to approach their client's issue from many different 'angles' and raise the probability of success.

Hypnotherapists often find that they have a lot of success with certain types of issues—mine being stress and anxiety. So that would be a really poignant question for you to ask a potential therapist. Some tell you that their strength lies in helping clients with weight management or smoking, others may feel more attuned to working specifically with men or women. For this reason, I would encourage you to phone a few hypnotherapists in your area and, as you chat to them and ask your questions, also note whether you feel a rapport grow . . . I believe this to be an important part of the equation for success as well.

Part 2

The quick & easy way to overcome your anxiety

CHAPTER 4

MY HYPNOTHERAPY

*Hypnosis creates the divide between the conscious
and subconscious minds offering the opportunity of a
direct-line into the subconscious mind. Hypnotherapy,
therefore, is affecting change in a positive way
once you know the subconscious is listening.*

Clients can experience *immense* problems in their day-to-day
life because of their issue, and are surprised to learn that
their subconscious mind is happily oblivious to the fact
there's even a problem.

'How can this be?' you ask. 'I'm tearing my hair out trying to cope
with the anxiety I go through every day!' Well, that's because the
subconscious' attention is focused on doing its job of enacting all of
your automatic responses and keeping auto-pilot running smoothly.
It thinks it's doing a *wonderful* job! It's job is a bit like a juke box . . .
for example:

*You overhear someone make a negative comment about
your hair, the subconscious recognises that someone has*

*said something not very nice, and acknowledges that as
a result you're feeling self-conscious. Consequently, it
pushes the 'I'm feeling judged' button, and you'll play
the same record you've always played whenever you've
felt judged. You'll blush and feel like you're not good
enough. As a result you think to yourself, 'I must book
an appointment with the hair-dresser tomorrow!'*

*Someone else, who has their own unique and entirely
different set of records in their juke box, may encounter the
same scenario but their record might be one of defiance.
They may think 'how dare you make a judgement of me!'
stand up taller and give a 'who do you think you are' kind
of a look, before flicking their hair and striding off. In fact,
you could have ten different people encounter the same
scenario and each would play a slightly different record.*

As I said, the subconscious mind is so focused on its own record collection, pushing all the right buttons at the right time, and playing the same records over and over again, that it doesn't notice anything wrong.

Putting It All Together

So, as a hypnotherapist helping each client to make changes, it's important I take into consideration the basic workings of their mind and how this has contributed to their issue. Each client has their own unique combination of automatic responses and belief systems that drive their behaviour. Their subconscious isn't aware that there is a problem and is resistant to change (and so needs some *very* good reasons to even think about changing).

In addition to these factors, I also have a personal belief that to help someone as completely as I can, <u>firstly</u>, we should endeavour to find <u>why</u> their symptoms exist.

We shouldn't *just* be focusing on eliminating the symptoms of their troublesome automatic behaviour, we should be turning our attention to what created them . . . *'The Cause'.*

I guide my clients through a process that I feel takes into consideration all of these aspects . . . so I help them to:

- Identify their 'world' and how they see it, and how they operate within it.
- Awaken their subconscious mind to the reality of the problem and how it's affecting the client's life.
- Show their subconscious that there's a more beneficial way of doing things, so as to give it a reason and desire to change.
- De-clutter the built-up negativities.
- Find the 'cause' of what created their particular problematic issue in the first place.
- Neutralise the 'cause' so it can't continue to re-trigger the old automatic behaviour.
- Re-program the subconscious with repetitive positive suggestion.

Making The Change—What To Expect

All aspects are as important as each other in order to make the change as complete as possible. Yet, as a hypnotherapist I can't guarantee that change will be made or that it will be permanent, but I will certainly try to be as thorough as possible to ensure the likelihood of long-term change is as great as possible.

Change is obviously **the** thing that clients want to achieve when they come for hypnotherapy. Still, everyone's expectations are different. Some don't feel that it will work, but give it a go anyway, while others expect to walk out of the office after the first session and for everything to be spontaneously and radically different.

Change can be sudden and quick for some, but for many it can be subtle and continue to occur weeks and months after our work together. When shifting a profound and in-grained self-belief system, many other things may have to shift to accommodate the big change that we're asking for, and as such, I always ask for it to be done 'safely, sensibly and comfortably', to ensure that the client can cope with it. The subconscious may also need a little time to figure out how to accommodate the new changes.

Ultimately, change through hypnotherapy is generally much quicker than with the more cognitive modalities of psychology and counselling, which I still believe have a valid place in helping people understand themselves, however, in my experience . . .

Hypnotherapy is proving to be an extremely effective
and quick form of making profound life changes.

CHAPTER 5

INFORMATION GATHERING

The first part of the process I use, is 'Information gathering'. It's an <u>essential</u> part of the process, it allows me to 'tune in' to the essence of a client as well as allowing me to compile a 'map' of the client.

The questions I ask are aimed at finding information like:

- How does the issue affect their lives—past and present?
- How do they view themselves and their personality, including good and bad traits?
- How do they view those around them?
- How did they view their parents, siblings, school and peers whilst growing up?
- What they <u>don't</u> want (what they want to change)?
- What they <u>do</u> want (their goals)?

Listening Carefully

I find that as a client talks, several things start to become apparent. They start to say the same sort of things about themselves, but in a number of different ways and contexts, and as they continue to answer my questions and tell me about their issue, their existence starts to 'leak out' by the words they use. This allows me to see the belief systems they hold about themselves and how their world 'works'. Belief systems always exist, even if clients aren't consciously aware of them.

The information they tell me about how they saw their parents and their childhood is vital and provides the foundation of our work together. It's so important to know if a client saw their mum as warm and cuddly or cold and aloof, and whether they remember their dad playing cricket in the back garden and giving them attention, or if they only remember him coming home from the pub and arguing with their mum most nights. This is the very stuff that 'is' their world, it creates the belief systems they carry through their lives and therefore affects everything they do.

For example, they might be someone who learnt from their warm and cuddly mum that they were cherished and wanted, and consequently find themselves being generally confident, fitting in easily to most situations and having mutually respectful relationships in their life. Alternatively, they may have learned from their absent father, who never did anything with them and never praised them, that they weren't really worth spending time with. This resulted in them tending to gravitate towards people who treat them badly or reject them, and having no motivation to achieve anything because 'what's the point?' After all, they learnt that nobody seems to care whether they achieve anything or not.

Perception Is Everything

It's important to outline here that a client's perception of childhood events is not always factual. Their perception could have been quite different from reality, especially if they experienced an event that became the reason for them focusing so much on one particular aspect of home life. For example, Dad might have been a normal, caring and loving father, but one incident where he ignored his son because he was too busy, could have initiated the son's perception that Dad *never* had any time for him, resulting in his perspective that his brother got all the attention.

It's actually irrelevant what the facts are, because if that's what the client remembers, then the chances are, the subconscious has created its belief systems and automatic behaviours around this way of thinking—whether it was true or not.

Compiling The Client's Map

Through working with so many people and learning the relevant questions to ask initially, I am able to determine where to focus my ongoing questioning. The answers highlight the basic essence of how a person sees themself and their world, which is now a contributing factor to their issue.

I specifically question clients on the dominant emotions they consistently feel, because it's always an emotion that triggers the automatic response. Especially important to know is the consistent behaviour or experiences that pop up periodically throughout their life that seem to form a pattern. As I continue through my questioning and write down the answers, I start to form a 'map' of that person. My map then starts to highlight the obvious connections, repetitions and cycles between all the elements noted and after a while, the core of the issue will often start to 'jump out of the page'.

Never Presume

I use this 'map' only as an aid though, I never pre-empt what underlies a client's issue—I leave that totally up to the subconscious mind, because it's the *only* one who truly knows why the issue is there, the cause of it and how it plays out in their life—often under the surface.

Useful Information

So, why do I bother gathering all this information if I don't use it to find all the definitive answers? I use it to firstly find out exactly how the client's issue is *negatively* affecting their day-to-day life. I need to know their turmoil, their worries and their fears so that I can tell the subconscious mind all about it when I finally have its 'ear'. After I've done that, I also tell it exactly what it is that the client is aiming for, detailing the positive changes they want to enjoy and any aspirations and dreams that can be used as motivation for change.

The next part of the process is to relay all of this information to the subconscious.

CHAPTER 6

SHOW THE SUBCONSCIOUS MIND THE EXISTING PROBLEM

T he subconscious' primary role is as 'protector' and therefore its basic instinct is likely to 'kick in' a lot more if it feels that something negative is going on.

By this stage in the first session, I will already have gleaned information from my client about how their issue affects them on both a practical level and an emotional level—particularly the *consistent* emotion their problem evokes in them. I might have asked questions such as: 'Do you constantly get angry at the slightest thing?' or, 'Are you swamped by guilt even when you haven't done anything wrong?' This enables me to identify the relevant emotion that sparks off the behaviour, and then relay this information back to the subconscious in its own *emotional language*.

So once the person is hypnotised, I describe to the subconscious in detail, how their personal belief systems and automatic responses are affecting them negatively . . . whether it be how they go through their day-to-day lives trying to maintain their belief system by eating too much chocolate because they think of themselves as 'big-boned', or how they enact their automatic response of starting arguments with their partner as a way to sabotage relationships because they think that they're 'not good enough' to be loved.

Other types of information that I'll reflect back to the subconscious stem from how they *perceive* their parents treated them when they were younger or how they viewed their school life whilst growing up, including any teachers that stood out and school friends they spent time with, or any bullying that went on.

From my observations, it seems that many an issue has been sparked off in the school playground or classroom. Children often say whatever is on their minds, however hurtful it might be, but equally it appears that teachers can also say and do the most potentially damaging things . . . some comments appear to be totally harmless and you'd never imagine they'd start such life-long anxiety, but others are clearly downright wrong!

You'll notice I've use the word 'perceive' again . . . In your own life, you may have encountered how you 'perceived' your childhood to be totally different from your siblings. As an adult you may have been reminiscing with your brother and sister over a bottle of wine one night, and listened in total disbelief as your brother describes a particular event, but in a *completely* different way to how you remembered it. You then start arguing, both of you swearing your versions are absolutely right!

Siblings often remember their childhoods differently to each other, especially in as much as how they saw their parents and how their parents treated them. Consequently, I'm sure you can see, that even siblings brought up in the same household can have completely different issues and personality traits from one another.

Getting In Touch With Emotion

This individual perception of past events doesn't just include the practical and logical 'facts'. Although when we remember it and run through it again from the conscious mind's point of view, it's usually only the 'facts' that we re-connect with. However, when I reflect the problem back to the subconscious during hypnosis, the emotion surrounding the event is often felt too. In fact, the level of emotion that they encounter can be intense because we're really getting to the core of that emotion. People are generally scared of strong emotion, and so I always talk about this aspect before we commence hypnosis. If they feel a strong wave of emotion, their natural instinct might be to open their eyes, sit upright and then want to run out of the office! But it's important to understand that this emotion hasn't 'just' appeared because of what we're doing, it's been there for a long time, probably buried, and suppressed and bubbling under the surface contributing to their issue. Therefore, what better time to look at it than whilst we're in a safe environment in which to work?

Emotional Highs And Lows

I personally feel that allowing the subconscious mind to experience a negative emotion is as necessary as feeling the good ones. Yes, the person may cry and feel upset for a while, but then that feeling will subside and they'll start to feel better. This, I believe, shows the subconscious mind that emotions are not necessarily to be feared, but instead to be felt, acknowledged, and then let go of.

We, as humans are here to experience *all* emotions, the good and the bad—not just feel the good ones and ignore and bury the bad ones, which, is what we so often do. Additionally, this concept that 'only' good feelings should be experienced, can lead to a person adopting the concept that 'everything' is wrong if a bad feeling creeps in. Ironically, that person will get 'stuck' in the bad feelings they're so afraid of. When this happens, hopelessness can be overwhelming, which can lead to depression.

A classic way of ignoring the bad, of course, is to numb the mind with things such as alcohol and drugs . . . after all, when we have them, we don't have to feel the bad stuff. Of course, the more we do this, the more we become fearful of the buried emotions, then the more we need to numb them again . . . and there the vicious cycle begins! All of which only goes to show how the emotion felt during this part of a client's session is actually an important and beneficial part of the process; and connecting with it allows them to feel it and consequently wake the subconscious mind up to the fact that it's there.

The subconscious is now aware that we have a problem! But we certainly don't want to leave it there, because waking it up to the problem, but not giving it a solution, means that it will have to find one for itself—and with it having no logic, it's choice might not necessarily be a better one! Although the likelihood is that the subconscious would probably just give up fairly quickly on finding an alternative, and choose the easy option of going back to its old way of doing things.

CHAPTER 7

SHOW THE SUBCONSCIOUS MIND THE BENEFITS OF CHANGE

I always find it interesting when I question the client at the beginning of our work together about what they want to achieve, because after focusing on the reams and reams of all the things they don't want, don't like and can't put up with anymore, when I ask them what they 'do' want, they often will look at me blankly. They then pause for a while and say 'I don't really know, I just don't want that lot anymore!'

Imagine Your Way To Happiness

But this part of the process—getting excited about a new way of doing things, and new exciting experiences to look forward to—has a lot to do with the success of a person's change. In fact, many of you reading this chapter may have read the odd book or two on the power of positive thinking, and, if you remember what I said earlier . . .

> *'The subconscious does not know the difference between reality and imagination,' then you may want to start to imagine yourself already being the way you want to be.*

Even in your day-to-day life, instead of getting consumed by your usual worrying thoughts that trigger your anxiety symptoms (since the subconscious doesn't know you're 'only' worrying—it thinks it's actually happening!) you can switch your thinking. Start to imagine what it would feel like doing all sorts of wonderful new things, and again, the subconscious will think your 'imaginings' are really happening. Do this often enough, and you can actually influence change. The consistency will attract the attention of the subconscious as it registers all the positive emotion and realises that it would be beneficial for you if it were to adapt.

Hypnosis gives this 'positive thinking process' extra *'oomph'* especially at this point of the proceedings when we've just told the subconscious about a big problem, and are straight away offering it a fantastic solution. The subconscious is well-known for being a bit lazy when it comes to having to change, so visualising like this makes its job a lot easier. Hypnosis allows the new imaginings to be planted more deeply than they would with conscious thinking alone, and greatly increases the chance of them being accepted because you don't have the conscious mind actively getting in the way and saying, 'Nope . . . I can't see that working!'

How To Decide What You <u>Do</u> Want?

So, if I find my client is struggling to come up with some ideas of what they 'do' want, I might prompt them a little and say something like, 'Ok . . . if you woke up tomorrow and some miracle had happened over night, what would your day be like?' Usually, as a starting point, they'll say something like, 'I just want to be happy really'. But happiness to one person is something totally different to another—so it's important to discover what happiness is to them. I often prompt them by looking at what they *don't* want and then saying something like, 'OK . . . if you don't want to lay in bed at night worrying endlessly and unable to get to sleep, how would you like to feel instead?' After a bit of thought the client might say, 'Well then, I'd like to feel calm and relaxed generally, and be able to switch off my mind at night so I can get to sleep easily'. And straight away we have something positive to aim for. From there, I might go through a few more points in the same way and build up some great 'dreaming material'.

When I present this side of things to the subconscious mind, I endeavour to describe it in a way that enables the client to conjure up the *feelings* that go along with actually experiencing the desired changes. Remember, the subconscious needs us to talk to it in its own 'emotional' language as much as possible, or else we might as well be talking to it in Swahili!

Encouraging Conscious/Subconscious Teamwork

I also give the client homework. Once the dream, or the goal is 'planted' in the subconscious mind of new positive ways of 'doing' and 'feeling', the client is encouraged to nurture and feed the goal in order for it to be deep-rooted and to flourish and grow. Think of your imagination as the water for your new plant, and your feelings as the fertiliser.

Homework consists of the client re-imagining the positive goals as often as possible, but most importantly just before they go to sleep at night. This way, they are being consistent in thinking better thoughts, are being positive before they go to sleep, and are taking that positivity into sleep-time which is when the subconscious does much of its processing of the day and re-adjusting and re-arranging.

This is a great routine for clients to adopt on an ongoing basis—or, preferably, for life! I advise clients to get into the habit of being mindful of the 'good stuff' especially when going to bed at night. This provides a technique to actively 'kick-start' the process of thinking positively, thus avoiding getting swept away with the negativity they would normally find themselves focusing on at bedtime. I see many an insomnia-sufferer who can't get to sleep because of worrying thoughts keeping them awake for hours.

Hypnotherapist/Client Teamwork

Many people come to a hypnotherapist because they think it's the 'easy option': that they won't have to do *anything* at all, that it will be quick, with no effort on their part, and that they won't remember anything about it. Relatively speaking, clients do tend to have a lot less input than if they were undergoing therapy with a counsellor or psychologist for months on end, and some clients don't do any of the things I ask them to do between sessions and can still have changes occur. But the more a client involves themself in the process, both during hypnosis (if they're able to) as well as the things I ask them to do in their daily life, the better results they're likely to have. (Different people will experience varying degrees of input during the actual hypnosis, because some might be more awake than those that go so deeply they tend to sleep through much of it).

But the reason a person comes for hypnotherapy is because they <u>want</u> to change, and the more they are part of the process rather than just being a bystander to their own change, the more thorough their success is likely to be. The degree of change could be disappointing for people who don't participate at all, i.e. they won't give me much information at the beginning of the work, or they don't do any of their homework. They may also be very happy to blame the hypnotherapist rather than look to themselves. As for those who actively try to prove that hypnotherapy is a load of rubbish—yes, people do come and see me to prove that I can't help them, so that it gives them the excuse to continue doing what they're doing and not making changes . . . well we won't go there!

I will often ask a client prior to booking a session with them if they are happy to come to hypnotherapy. This is because I do get people who come along because they were told to by their spouse, or they think they probably *should*, but deep down they don't really want to. I often have a wife who'll phone up on behalf of her husband wanting him to be 'fixed', yet when the husband walks in and I start talking to him, it's clear that he's 'quite happy the way he is, thank you very much!' thereby making change unlikely. Indeed, I have no right to try to change people when they don't want to be changed. So I always endeavour to speak to the person coming for the therapy to ascertain how serious they are about making changes, and even turn them away if I feel there's not much point in continuing.

I'm sure you can see that hypnotherapy is <u>not</u> all about the 'hypnotherapist', it's also <u>very much</u> about the client and their participation in the process, together with the hypnotherapist's particular skills and techniques. The effective hypnotherapist knows how to use the tools in their tool bag to unlock the door to each client's unique answers, so as to tailor the process to them, and actually help them achieve the changes that they want.

Up to this point of the process,

- We have presented the subconscious mind with the problem and, hopefully inspired it to enact its role of 'protector'.

- and then immediately got it excited enough to aspire it to change by giving it the solution—now we're getting somewhere!

These first two parts of the process are all included in the first hypnotherapy session and then to round off this session, it's good to 'de-clutter' and make way for new stuff!

CHAPTER 8

DE-CLUTTERING THE SUBCONSCIOUS MIND

I t's good to 'clear out the cobwebs', we can all benefit by doing this from time to time. I have clients who come back maybe 3-6 monthly just to have their 'maintenance de-cluttering session', because life seems to have a habit of dumping more and more stuff in the bin!

Carrying Around a Life-Time's Worth of Negative 'Stuff'

Over time, we have many experiences throughout our day-to-day lives and as a result we collect negativities from those experiences. We might, for example, experience anger that we feel is inappropriate to express, so we hold on to it, and squish it down with all the other negative emotions collected over time and suppressed—and it all builds up. Much of what we adopt in this way, isn't always 'ours' as such, but is often a result of taking on other people's 'stuff' too . . .

either they've forced it upon us to help *them* feel better, or we've gotten so used to taking on everyone else's issues and negativities that we just don't know how to stop.

> *I think of this process a bit like using a trash can . . . you keep piling things into it, but it's only 'so big' and can only take 'so much' before the lid won't contain it and bits start to fall out.*

Mid-Life Crisis

It's no coincidence that many of my clients are around the 40-50 year age range. I've come to recognise that mid-life crisis is merely an overflowing of the bin. It's quite common for me to have a 45 year old male client sit down in the chair . . . a man who's been taught that *'men don't cry'* and must just *'get on with it!'* . . . and they'll sit there for a while, and probably the first thing they'll say is, 'I don't know why I'm here really.' Then after a long silence, they'll add, 'I just keep feeling quite teary lately which is not like me at all' . . . and 'I've been getting quite snappy and the wife has had enough. I sort of feel like, what's the point?'

I think that we go through our lives putting up with things, suppressing things and ignoring things until we get to a certain age when we can't ignore them anymore. I believe that we are here to learn about our internal issues so we can address them, work through them and 'grow'. But the problem is that we get completely side-tracked by having busy lives . . . or, we create our busy lives as a way of completely side-tracking ourselves so we can avoid looking at our issues, let alone find a way to deal with them. The work I do with clients, I feel, helps them to, firstly, empty the bin, and secondly, find out . . . *finally* . . . what's causing the bin to get so full up.

New Technology Overloading
Our Children's Trash Cans

Taking into consideration the concept of the overflowing trash can, it's an interesting thing to ask the question, 'How will today's technology contribute to our children's issues in the future?' How much quicker will their bins start to overflow because they have so much technology at their fingertips . . . every moment of every day . . . that does the best job *ever* in the history of evolution to encourage them to avoid processing normal human emotions. In addition to this, it trains them from a very young age to be continually bombarded and overloaded with stimuli. It comes at them from all angles, every moment of the day, and even sometimes through the night. I even found my own children thinking it was alright to go off to sleep listening to Metallica pumping through their MP3 earpieces.

Through talking with my younger clients, it's become apparent that many of them are already in the habit of *never* switching off their gadgets or spending any quiet time alone with their feelings to try and process them. They are continually swamped in computers, phones and play music in their ear 24 hours a day—to say nothing of 'electronic socialising' as opposed to having face-to-face conversations with their friends. What happens when people miss out on the important step of processing the emotional content of both sides of a conversation? What effect will this global change in socialising and lack of processing of emotions have on society? I feel the likelihood is that anxiety levels will rise.

Let's consider the modern-day conversation . . . It's a lot easier to not have to feel any responsibility for the words you bestow on another person if you don't have to face them while you're doing it. Firstly, you miss out on what it takes to have the courage to speak the words, then secondly, to discover what emotions the words evoke in both yourself and the other person once you've delivered them. There is also the added confusion that because of the absence of emotion, the receiver of a text or email has more chance of misinterpreting the intended meaning. I feel that socialising through electronic media almost absolves the participants from their responsibility within a conversation. It's as if they have a very basic part of their human learning experience of 'social interaction' missing, and therefore, when they do find themselves in a, what most people might consider to a be fairly normal social situation, they are completely panicked by the feelings of anxiety that it brings.

We don't know, as yet, what the consequences will
be of living in this technological age and how it
will affect us as a human race in the long term.

Anyway—I digress—back to the plot!

Releasing

So, to help the client offload all this 'stuff' built-up in their trash can, we utilise that previously mentioned nugget of information, *'the subconscious doesn't know the difference between imagination and reality,'* to enable the client to visualise themselves throwing away all the acquired rubbish.

The time spent talking with the client before hypnosis allows me to be specific when attaching many of the negatives they talked about to the things they throw away. For example, I might say something like: 'Imagine that you're throwing away all the self-doubt you've acquired over the years . . . especially the self-doubt that might have been given to you in your early years when you remember your dad saying that you were useless.'

This part of the process can be emotional for the client and sometimes there's an obvious look of relief on their face as they release something that's been with them for a long time. Often when I talk to the client after this first session and we discuss the 'de-cluttering' part of the proceedings, it becomes apparent how they've embraced the opportunity of off-loading their baggage. Their extra enthusiasm can 'turbo-boost' the power of their imagination and contribute to the effectiveness of this part of the process.

At this point, we've achieved a fair amount, and this 'de-cluttering' concludes the hypnosis part of the first session. After bringing the client out of hypnosis, we spend some time talking about what they experienced whilst they were 'under'. For example, how they experienced the actual feelings of being hypnotised and then specifically what they visualised and what they felt as I guided them through all the different parts of the process. I then discuss with them what they can expect between now and the next session and then send them away for about a week to see what happens.

What Will Happen After This Session?

So what can they expect after having done all this work? Well, everyone has their own way of responding to the first session, but I've found that there seems to be a bit of a trend. The client will tend to have a few really good days where they find themselves feeling notably better, sometimes filled with a sense of euphoria or feeling pleasantly 'different' and with the realisation that maybe this hypnotherapy actually works! Slowly, though, they might feel themselves start to revert back to their usual demeanour, whatever that might be. This then triggers disappointment that things are sliding backwards—and they think to themselves, 'I knew it was too good to be true. I knew this wouldn't work',*@!* hypnotherapy!'

Because of this disappointment, I warn my clients that this 'slide backwards' may happen, otherwise they might be too disheartened to continue with the process. Change, especially significant and profound change, goes through a bit of an 'up and down' process—this is normal. In fact, sometimes the subconscious can actually get worse before it settles down and gets better. This is especially true for weight management clients who after two days might find themselves raiding the pantry every 15 minutes, licking everyone's plates clean at the dinner table and pinching ice creams from kids as they pass by in pushchairs!

Contrary to the way it's portrayed on the television, hypnotherapy is rarely about the hypnotherapist saying something <u>once</u> and it being adopted instantly and permanently.

Repetition Is Usually Needed

The thing to remember here, is that as humans, we are 'designed' in a way that means **repetition is often an important component of how we learn**. At this stage of the hypnotherapy process however, the subconscious mind has only been told the new goal *once*. Compare that with the example of learning to ride a bike when you were a youngster. You certainly weren't told how to do it once and then just jumped on the bike and away you went, *no!* I would hazard a guess that there were a few scraped arms and knees involved along the way as you tried, time and time again, to learn how to balance, pedal and steer all at the same time. Even then, just when you thought you'd mastered it, didn't you crash into the nearest tree? Still, you kept trying, again, and again, and again until eventually, *hey presto . . . you did it!* And from then on, it became completely automatic to you, so much so that you didn't even have to 'think' about how to ride your bike—you just did it. In fact, it became so accepted and automatic within your subconscious mind that you could get on a bike years—even decades later—and still just do it without thinking.

*And so it is with learning anything new . . . including how
to change from feeling anxious every time you think about
getting up to do some public speaking, to being able to get
up and confidently speak to a whole roomful of people.*

Clients' Responses Will Vary

Just like when you're learning anything, the norm is to experience a bit of 'up and down' during this process of hypnotherapy. However, some lucky people do find themselves responding quickly to positive new suggestions during hypnosis. I've had clients who have made almost instant changes and taken on every positive suggestion I've given them . . . but this is not the norm.

The number of sessions therefore that a client requires, depends on both the suggestibility of the client and the process the hypnotherapist uses. For example, I believe whole-heartedly that finding the 'cause' of anyone's issue is *essential*, and attempting to include all the elements required to find the cause and then re-program them, in just one session, would likely be 'overload'. And for those clients whose subconscious requires lots of repetition to adopt the new positive suggestions, further sessions may be needed to just *repeat, repeat, repeat!*

There are, however, hypnotherapists who specialise in 'quitting smoking in one session—guaranteed!' so I'm sure there is something out there for everyone. Each person has their own philosophy on these types of things and I suggest that clients choose the hypnotherapist that they most relate to, because even though I'm passionate about 'finding the cause', some people think it's just not something they're 'up for', preferring just to have their issue 'taken away'. As you may have guessed, I'm all for being aware of your 'stuff' because I believe that:

Self-knowledge is a powerful thing!

CHAPTER 9

FINDING THE CAUSE
OF YOUR ANXIETY

Finding 'the cause', to me, is like finding the
key that unlocks the answer to your issue.

Not all hypnotherapists feel comfortable delving into finding the *specific* cause of the anxiety or issue and so may, instead, simplify this part of the process by encouraging a client to simply 'let go of *anything*' connected to the issue. Much of their follow-on work would then evolve around lots of repetitive, positive suggestion to help reprogram automatic behaviour. (Indeed, both therapists *and* clients, should always be entirely comfortable with the process). But personally, it doesn't seem right to me to just try to make 'something' go away without knowing what it is that we are trying to get to disappear . . . Isn't this just another way of avoiding what's really going on? And what has the client learnt about themselves if the hypnotherapist just 'takes it all away' for them?

Not Knowing What You Fear,
Fuels Your Anxiety

It seems to me that avoiding and suppressing negative emotions induces a sense of fear around them; a person might know something is there, bubbling away under the surface, but daren't look at it—and they don't know quite what it is or even *exactly* what it's doing.

I feel that many negative issues are triggered by this sense of often-unidentified fear or pain that people carry around with them. As a result, the subconscious mind goes through life trying to protect them from it—mostly by skirting around it. It does this in all sorts of ways:

- by being excessively busy so as not to have time to acknowledge it,
- drinking and taking drugs to numb it,
- and eating for comfort in the hope of feeling better in spite of it . . . just to name a few.

You Could Acquire New Anxiety Symptoms

Now, it's all very well to 'take away' something by asking the subconscious mind to just 'let it go'. But, if it hasn't been identified, how does someone know if the subconscious has actually let it go? And if it hasn't been released, could it manifest in other ways if the current symptoms disappear?

I had a client come to see me, and during our initial session of information-gathering, she mentioned that she'd been to a hypnotherapist two years prior to her visit with me and that the hypnotherapist had successfully helped her to give up smoking. Having moved across state, she was coming to me now because she was feeling more and more anxiety in her day to day life and she didn't know why. At the age of 40, she had started to experience anxiety when flying, which was a problem since her job required her to fly virtually every week. This was a complete mystery to her since she'd never experienced it before. She'd now got to the point where she had been to the doctors for a certificate to excuse her from work. I asked her when she thought her anxiety had started and she said 'about two years ago'. Aha! A remarkable coincidence? I think not!

I believe that whatever anxiety the smoking had been helping her to cope with, was now coming out in other ways because she didn't have the smoking to rely on. How many people have you heard of giving up smoking, then suddenly eating so much they start to put on weight? I worked with this client on finding the cause to her anxiety (which went way back to a childhood experience), and after finishing the rest of our work together, I received a grateful phone call from her after her first shift back at work to say the flight had gone well, and, as far as I know, no new symptoms have arisen since.

So, one of the reasons that I'm adamant about finding the cause is because it seems to me that if I don't, it will stay sitting there below the surface, waiting for another way to express itself.

The More You Know About Yourself, The Better You Can Be

The other important reason for finding the cause, as I mentioned, is for you, as a person, to learn something about yourself that will hopefully have a positive effect on your life. Self-knowledge is a powerful thing. If you know that a past event you'd possibly forgotten about or had just filed in the *'oh well, shit happens!'* box, had actually had a profound effect on you—this knowledge could answer some of your questions. Why you feel so mortally wounded whenever someone criticises you? Or, why you can't seem to ever find the confidence to fulfil your dreams and be a success? This new awareness about yourself can firstly help you to make sense of why you do what you do, and secondly, help you to direct your focus in the process of positive change.

When 'the cause' happens, the memory of it is stored in the subconscious mind (this is where your long term memory is) and from that moment on, everything shifts slightly as if you now look at the world differently to how you did before. You could liken it to looking at the world through a pair of glasses, but 'the cause' puts a filter on your glasses resulting in everything which happens to you being viewed through the filter first, altering your perception.

Child vs Adult Perception

Most people probably think that 'the cause' must be some awful, deep, dark secret for it to have created so much angst in their life, but interestingly, it's often something exceedingly trivial. The emotion felt at the time of the event, however, in the young mind of a child, would have been noted by the subconscious as being significant. One of the key things to remember is that when you're older, reflecting back on your childhood memories, you're mostly doing so using your conscious, logical mind and as such, more than likely leaving the emotional content out of the equation. In other words, you might 'remember' the emotion that was there, but not 'feel' it.

As you reminisce over a specific childhood memory with your *adult mind*, you're likely to trivialise it. By now, you no doubt have a greater understanding of why the event happened, and why certain people did what they did. These are all perspectives that you didn't have at the time you were actually experiencing it, but will have you filing it away and grading it as 'not so bad' in the grand scheme of your life. As a child, however, experiencing it at the time, in full techni-color and with the emotion dial turned up to '11', that wasn't the case at all.

As a child you'd have been consumed by the emotion of the 'here and now' and wouldn't have had the greater awareness from your 'accumulated life experiences' to justify why someone was upsetting you. All you knew was that you were in the centre of your own Universe, and all you could see was what was going on immediately around you and that you were scared, upset or hurt in some way.

Clients often come to a session armed with a past traumatic event that they are *convinced* is the cause of their anxiety. However, if that event occurred *after* their automatic behaviour had already been created by a prior and relatively trivial event, they can be surprised to learn what the 'real cause' is. The traumatic event is certainly part of the equation, but effectively what it's really done is simply amplified or re-sensitised the initial cause so that its effect becomes noticeable.

Auto-Pilot Is Set In The Early Years

This is why someone might come to me and understandably think that their particular issue only started in their 30s because it was at the age of 32 that their marital relationship fell apart and they noticed the changes. But, in reality, that event simply re-sensitised the automatic behaviour of say, getting angry as a reaction to feelings of rejection. I've found that most people's automatic behaviours are created during the early years of between 0 and 10 years and occasionally through to the early teens. (I've noticed that ages 5 and 7 seem to be poignant years for setting up behaviour patterns). So when you think about that, your automatic behaviours and self-belief systems are all in place by the age of about 10, so you don't change much of what you do after that age.

*Let's say 'the cause' is the first time someone insulted you
about the way you looked and you got upset and felt self-
conscious. This might have happened, at say, seven years
old. The subconscious might have decided, as a result, that
the best way to protect you both at the time of the cause
and automatically in the future, is to get you away from
certain similar social situations. So now you look at the
world through your 'filter' and see that people can judge you
harshly, and that's proved to be scary! As a result, as you
grow up, you become someone who's generally introverted
and doesn't join in much . . . and maybe over time, things
get worse as you continue wearing the filter on your glasses.
You might also have experienced a few 're-sensitising' events
along the way that have alarmed your subconscious so
much so, that now, at say the age of 25 years old, it's on red
alert to the possibility that <u>everyone</u> you meet is thinking
something derogatory about you. A response that causes
overwhelming feelings of anxiety since the subconscious
enacts its 'flight or fight' response to get you out of danger
from being around all these threatening judgemental people!
Remember, through all of this, you have little or no logical
conscious input into whether you want to feel and act that
way . . . so no wonder you get confused and feel stuck!*

The obvious answer to me, is to find 'the cause' that's adhered itself to your glasses and effectively peel it off, and allow yourself to look at the world in a different way, with clearer vision. This starts to give you back choice . . . choice over your actions. If you're aware of 'the cause', and can recognise yourself reacting in the way you've always done before—out of habit, probably by now—you can 'stand back' from yourself. Then, with your new knowledge, fully recognise that what you would normally do is completely connected with one particular past event and has absolutely no connection to the present time, allowing your conscious mind to use that knowledge and have a greater input into *choosing* what to do this time. This is the conscious part of the equation of change. Our aim is to finally get the conscious and subconscious working together, not against each other.

Regression—
The Tool To Re-Connect With The Past

I've found that regression helps the client to re-visit a past event and to re-connect to it in a way that allows them to notice, <u>for the first time consciously and logically</u>, the subconscious perspective of the event. Then they recognise for themselves that they've carried this focus and associated emotions on a subconscious level ever since, and that they are constantly re-triggering their subconscious mind to activate the anxiety that has developed because of it.

I use regression to enable people to connect with 'the cause'. Regression is asking the subconscious mind to effectively go back in time and 're-connect' with a memory. When clients attend this session armed with a few memories that they're convinced simply *must* be the cause, I tell them to put all logic aside. This is the subconscious mind we're dealing with—there's no logic here! Sure enough, in my experience and to the client's surprise, the past event that *is* 'the cause' is usually something totally different.

(Please note: If you, as a client, want to work with your hypnotherapist in the way outlined on these pages of 'regressing to find the cause', I strongly advise you to locate one that has the relevant experience of working in this way.)

The Subconscious Knows The Answer

When I tell clients that the information is going to come from their subconscious, I think they expect some voice to emerge from the heavens to talk for them. But I tell them, 'No, it will be your own voice and it will just feel as if you're chatting away to me with your eyes closed'. Even though clients sometimes get nervous because they don't know what to expect, surprisingly they get more worried that they might not find the cause at all. Before we start, I explain that they will be talking back to me, but that the information will be sourced from their subconscious mind and then filtered through to their conscious awareness so that they can see and feel it again. It will feel similar to me asking them to remember their last holiday and describing to me what they did.

Clients often start off with a completely blank mind for quite some time, and then they tend to get what I call the 'trickle effect' of information coming through. They might, for example, just remember a house they lived in when they were eight years old, or somebody might pop into their head, but at this point, they're probably not quite sure why. They could even just start off feeling an emotion which seems to have come from nowhere, but when I ask them to focus on whatever it is they are seeing or feeling, additional information will come through enabling them to make more sense of it, which is when a more complete picture starts to form.

Sometimes the subconscious will visit several events on its way back to 'the cause' . . . I call this the 'stepping stone' method. I quite like this particular method as it offers lots of information, indicating the 'theme' running through all the different memories. I also ask the subconscious mind, whilst we're looking at a cause, to recognise how it is still carrying this out in the person's life and at the same time to recognise the need for change since their life is different now that they are older. So, as they're experiencing the memory from childhood I will ask the client to recognise the *'familiarity of feeling'* and acknowledge that they still feel that way today. This is usually a massive '*aha* moment!', because it is our feelings that we instantly associate with, and the recognition is usually profound when we fully realise where they started.

While We Are Here, What Else Can We Learn?

During the regression, I will ask the subconscious mind to share general insights into the situation, thereby allowing the client to become aware of any connections between all the different elements of the issue. It's enlightening to have access to the wealth of information that the subconscious has stored, and I get to see the '*oh my word!*' look on the client's face as they start to find the answers to their questions.

Another interesting trend I've seen happening is that the subconscious will actually take the client back to happy and totally unrelated memories first. It seems to happen when the client needs to be reminded that they have, and therefore can in the future, experience positive feelings. I take my cue from the subconscious and emphasise these good memories and good feelings and 'cement' them in. I also ask the client to use these memories as a future tool to switch negative feelings to positive ones.

It's Usually Trivial

Clients are generally surprised at 'the cause' and often can't believe that such a seemingly trivial event has had such a huge impact on their life. But it's good to remember that when you were young, anything new was BIG and probably scary to your subconscious mind, forcing it to learn how to respond to the event and create your automatic behaviour to enable you to cope with it in the future. For example:

I had a client who, as a boy, used to go to his aunt and uncle's house most weekends. His aunt was generally a noisy, busy, 'shouty' kind of a woman, while his uncle was a quiet soul by all accounts. My client used to love spending time with his uncle in the garden helping him tend to his plants. One day though, when he was just three years old, he went outside before his uncle, and saw what he thought were weeds growing in the garden and proceeded to pull them up. His uncle came out, saw that he had, in fact, pulled out all of his lettuces, and his natural reaction was to shout at him. In the boy's experience, his uncle never shouted . . . Aunty, yes! . . . but not his uncle. The boy was <u>so</u> shocked. Something in his world as he knew it just changed, and the subconscious mind was unnerved by this new emotion of fear—so much so, that he ended up running away.

This event seemed quite trivial in the grand scheme of my client's life. However, at the age of three, to the subconscious mind, this event was anything but trivial. It was scary, things were different, and it didn't like it one bit! This was the *first time* his subconscious mind had experienced fear, and its way of dealing with it was to run. This then became his way of dealing with anything that he considered to be scary throughout his life.

The process I guide clients through ultimately enables them to experience 'the cause' for themselves. I see myself very much as the guide . . . I'm there to help <u>them</u> find <u>their</u> answers. This enables them to understand fully why they act the way they do, in a way that <u>they can see it and feel it for themselves.</u> Experiencing it in this way, contributes greatly, I believe, to making the changes clients want, while also acquiring some self-understanding and self-development along the way.

Regression—Fors And Against

A common view against regression comes from the standpoint of saving clients from re-living painful experiences. 'It was bad enough the first time, so why do it again?' Added to this, is the fear held by some hypnotherapists that their client could have an abreaction (which is an uncontrollable emotional outburst), and they might not be able to stop it!

I can understand why someone might think this, but I still feel that not truly acknowledging the original experience and the emotions that were felt at the time is still encouraging the subconscious to be fearful of it. My clients often do feel great waves of emotion, 80% of them cry during the work we do together, and yes, some *do* sob uncontrollably for a while, but I have regressed hundreds and hundreds of clients and I haven't had *one* that has felt worse for having had experienced the emotion. Results range from clients feeling *so* much better, lighter and sometimes euphoric with a real sense of '*oh . . . now I understand!*' and at worse, they are a little pensive about what they've experienced.

Once again, the key to ensuring a positive outcome, especially for those who are scared of emotions and used to avoiding them, is in explaining to the client what to expect *before* we enter into this part of the work. I tell them that although the emotions might initially seem overwhelming, I'll guide them through the process of releasing and re-balancing them, which will help them feel calm again. Those that do experience high levels of emotion are often the ones who claim to have had the most profound experience . . . For some, it's a *huge* relief, as if a massive weight has been lifted off their shoulders.

Often, clients who'd previously shied away from
emotion, recognise, through the experience of regression,
the benefit of having finally connected to it.

At the end of the regression session we discuss what they've experienced during this part of the process, and I'm always interested to find out how the client feels about what 'the cause' was. Sometimes people are completely surprised at what it was, sometimes they half expected it. Usually though, it's something that they do remember, but never considered it as being an important event in their life.

> *So, it is through experience that I stand by my belief that using regression to find 'the cause' is without doubt the way to help people overcome their issues and make changes.*

> *This newly acquired <u>conscious</u> understanding, together with the hypnotherapist's positive reprogramming of the <u>subconscious mind,</u> means that finally, both parts of their mind are in tune with each other. When this is achieved, wonderful things can happen!*

CHAPTER 10

NEUTRALISING THE CAUSE OF YOUR ANXIETY

O nce a 'cause' has been pin-pointed, if we simply leave it sitting there at the forefront of your subconscious mind, it's still going to be the over-zealous trigger to your automatic response its always been. Therefore, the next stage I guide clients through, is what I call 'neutralising'.

'<u>Neutralise</u>' it, so that it no longer
acts as a primary trigger.

Now this is where we need to remember, yet again, the importance of: *'the sub conscious mind doesn't know the difference between reality and imagination'.* Whilst in hypnosis, I guide the client to imagine doing various things to help neutralise their own individual 'cause'.

Who Is Responsible?

The cause nearly always involves somebody else (in fact, I haven't come across one yet that hasn't). It's 'the other person' involved in the event or experience that alerted the subconscious mind to the fact that it was experiencing an uncomfortable emotion for the first time—and this 'someone' didn't only have an acting role in this memory that would be playing over and over again like a movie loop . . . they had the starring role! This is because we respond *emotionally* to what people do or say and how they treat us . . . even if it's not directly. For example, if the experience that caused your issue was falling down a deep hole when you were five years old, although the experience and coinciding pain would have certainly magnified the situation, your emotional reaction would probably have been focused on: *'Mum should have been looking after me properly. How could she let this happen to me? Why is she not coming to get me out?'*

> *We always respond emotionally to how other people treat us . . . and it is the emotions that trigger off all automatic responses.*

Interestingly, the person the subconscious mind is 'blaming', is not necessarily the person the client consciously and logically would have singled out as the culprit. This is where, again, finding out the truth can mean that we can help neutralise the event in the *correct* way rather than assuming or guessing what we're dealing with. For example:

> *I had a client who had suffered sexual abuse at the hands of a male stranger whilst playing in a park at the age of six years old. To the complete surprise of the client, her subconscious was more focussed on the aunt*

who was looking after her at the time, than she was
focused on the abuser himself. For the subconscious
mind, the abuser was just a minor part of the equation,
while the level of anger towards her aunt was immense.
Her aunt failed to keep her safe and protect her and
should have been watching her more closely . . . this new
information was a complete surprise, but pointed us in
the right direction of where to focus the neutralisation.

How The Cause Can Create
A Life-Long Belief System

Embroiled in the event that caused an issue . . . including the emotion experienced and the consequential automatic response . . . is the possibility of the creation of a long-term, deep-rooted belief system. Let's go through a whole example of what can happen . . .

As a child, you are asked to stand up and read in front of the
class, and maybe you trip up on a few words here and there.
The teacher then berates you in front of everyone for not
having practiced your reading and the class bully initiates
laughter from the whole class by making a joke of it all.

Several things are at play here. Firstly, <u>in your mind</u>, the teacher, by pointing out your inability to read properly in front of everyone, is *to 'blame'* for causing a belief system of 'I'm a failure'. This 'belief' stays with you for life, it's the way you look at yourself, it affects everything you do and you find yourself constantly attaching that 'I just can't do it' attitude to most things you try in life.

While the bully, by making a stupid remark, made you feel self-conscious in front of everyone, is *'to blame'* for causing you to have no self-confidence, something that again stays with you for life. In the future, whenever you feel someone looking at you, your automatic response is to assume they're thinking negative things.

The class's reaction of laughing and ridiculing you, causes an extremely uncomfortable feeling which only magnifies the whole event as one that the subconscious remembers intensely as not liking one bit!

Therefore, because of that classroom experience, you now carry the aforementioned belief systems and automatic behaviours around with you in your every-day life, although not necessarily consciously. Fast forward a good few years, you're an adult at work and your boss asks if you'll do a presentation at the upcoming board meeting, suddenly *'things'* start to happen!

On a conscious level you don't get too worried about the upcoming meeting because it's been years since the original event, and you've almost forgotten all about it consciously. Still, under the surface, your subconscious is suddenly alerted, it remembers that school experience like it was yesterday and specifically remembers that it was extremely scary and doesn't want to do it again!

It's nearly time for your presentation, you're in the boardroom surrounded by your work colleagues. You might be sitting there quite calmly at first, but as you start to recognise that it's almost your turn to speak, the subconscious then goes into 'protection-mode'. It wants to protect you from this potential up-coming threat, and so initiates the 'flight or fight' response, because as far as it's concerned, the only thing to save you from this scary ordeal is to scarper! So it gets the body ready to flee! You, meanwhile, start to feel these changes taking place in your body, but consciously can't work out what's going on. Why can hear your heart pounding in your chest? Why are you struggling to breathe properly? Why are your palms getting

sweaty and why you have a sick feeling in your stomach?
By the time you have to stand up in front of everyone at the
meeting and speak, you can barely get the words out. You're
aware that everyone can see your hands are shaking as
you hold up your report to read out. You feel like you have
absolutely no control over your body and all this seems quite
bizarre and totally illogical. It doesn't make any sense at all!

And you're right, it doesn't make sense . . . but remember, the subconscious mind has no logic. Even though consciously and logically you know that standing up in front of a group of people and talking is not going to cause you any harm . . . you won't die, there will be no bolt of lightning striking you down, and your audience are very unlikely to throw stones at you . . . yet the subconscious mind just sees *danger!*

This then becomes an *'issue'*, firstly because you don't understand consciously and logically why the 'boardroom experience' would have happened. Secondly, because you don't have any control over your body during this experience, and therefore you worry about it happening again in the future. After all, your body could do whatever it wanted and you couldn't stop it—and what if people in the room noticed the tremble in your voice, or heard your stomach gurgling or your heart pounding in your chest? Surely they must have, because it sounded like someone playing the bongos to you!

Now you start to project this all forward on to similar events, which then becomes full-scale worry! Once we start on the 'worry merry-go-round', this is when it can escalate into a debilitating anxiety issue; somebody only needs to mention the phrase 'public speaking' and you can feel the tell-tale knot in the stomach . . . and it all kicks off again!

So, going back to the hypnotherapy process I guide clients through, so far we have regressed the client and identified the above scenario as 'the cause'. Great! Now we have something *specific* to work with that we can start to neutralise bit-by-bit.

> ***This doesn't mean pretending it didn't happen . . .***
> ***the subconscious mind remembers everything. But***
> ***we can work with it, re-frame it, shrink it down***
> ***and send it way back into the archives, labelling it***
> ***as 'unimportant' in the subconscious so it doesn't***
> ***get used as an ongoing primary trigger.***

In our scenario, we clearly have our two people to focus on who will be involved in neutralising the cause . . . the teacher and the bully. The subconscious will see these two people as prevalent characters in its awareness, my client may not even realise how deeply these two people have affected him/her. For example, as well as the already mentioned issues they've helped to create, there might also be an underlying awareness of being wary or intimidated by authority figures (teacher) or out-spoken, pushy people (the bully). The client may find they tend to shy away from similar types of people in their life, being drawn instead to more quiet, introverted-types.

Again, this is an example of the process that I use . . . allowing you to know yourself better. You might now be able to answer questions such as: Why you've married your spouse—because he fits the non-threatening, quietly-spoken character that the subconscious mind feels safe with. Why the office high-flyer just annoys you so much . . . because he's had to be outspoken and pushy to climb up the corporate ladder. Why you opted to be a researcher . . . because this means you get to sit in the corner office where no-one notices you, so you don't have to feel self-conscious.

So, how do we neutralise this part of 'the cause' so that the subconscious mind won't continue to focus on what the teacher and bully did? We can effectively 'let it go' by *forgiving them.*

Forgiveness

Firstly, before I talk about forgiveness, I'd like to go off on a bit of a tangent about this word 'blame' and what it means. I can see people reading this generally having either one of the following two opinions: Firstly, there'll be those that think, 'Great!' I can blame everyone else for all my problems—that let's me off the hook—I want to book an appointment *now!*' Then there will be those who say, 'You can't go around not 'owning' your stuff and blaming everyone else—you need to take responsibility for your actions!'

In my opinion there is an element of truth in both of these points of view. There are a few things to consider. The person who is to 'blame' simply *did* or *didn't* do something, or said or didn't say something that initiated an emotional response from the client and that the subconscious saw as negative. The person with the 'blame' label around their neck, might not even have done anything particularly bad or intentionally harmful . . . and it was that child's unique perception of the world that caused them to perceive whatever happened in this particular way.

In the early years, anything that the subconscious hasn't experienced before—even the little things—can seem scary. Many parents do things out of protection and love, but still, some of the things they do can unknowingly cause a negative response in their child's subconscious. Remember, parents are also driven by their automatic responses and behaviours which are a result of their own childhood experiences. It can be helpful to understand that if there had been another ten people present to witness 'the cause', then each of those ten people would have perceived and responded differently, to match their own unique way of looking at the world, derived from their individual life experiences up to that point in time.

The subconscious mind, from this point onwards however, remembers that person's involvement and remembers how it felt about it . . . and uses this frame of reference to help it consider what to do in future similar situations. The subconscious would most certainly have a heightened awareness of the element of the experience it didn't like, i.e. which personality trait that person had, and what they may have looked like. They would also have been aware of the surroundings at the time. Was it a closed-in space? Was it dark? All of these elements would be stored in the subconscious and any one of them could be 'the thing' that triggers off future automatic emotional responses. It doesn't matter whether the event was logically trivial or traumatic, the subconscious just sees it as 'the experience that is to blame'—or in other words 'the cause'.

> *If the subconscious is blaming someone else for*
> *'the cause', then does this let us 'off the hook'*
> *from taking responsibility for our 'stuff'?*

At the time of 'the cause', being so small, we rarely had much control over what did and didn't happen to us. I've had many a client who has struggled with not having 'a voice' when they were younger, not being acknowledged, asked how they felt or given a choice of what to do next. After all adults are bigger and we were conditioned to do what they say from a very early age. But as we get older, then our responsibility must be acknowledged when we *do* recognise that our behaviour is not OK, either by our own standards or by society's.

Similarly, within a relationship things may not be deemed acceptable—and where it all gets a bit confusing is when you get two individuals who have an issue within their relationship, then who is right? Often, nobody is actually 'right'—just *different*—but surely it's each person's responsibility within the relationship to identify and acknowledge how their behaviour is contributing to its breakdown. Responsible action would then be to keep the lines of communication open so as to find positive ways to bring around changes that will benefit the relationship.

OK, sorry for that little detour, but I think it's an important one, don't you?

Back to forgiveness and our schoolroom scenario. Essentially, as I've said, the subconscious mind is holding one *huge* grudge against these two people (the teacher and the bully), and *blaming* them for causing you so much pain and fear . . . despite the fact that consciously this past event doesn't really feature in the world's worst events in your life, and you certainly don't consider yourself to hold any conscious blame towards them because, in the grand scheme of things, they didn't really do much. Still, we have to placate the subconscious mind, and allow it to start letting this go somehow.

My next step would be to ask the client to imagine that these two people are standing in front of them right now. Firstly I would ask the client if there is anything they feel they would like to say to them. This enables them to finally have their 'voice' and be heard . . . they can verbalise how they felt at the time, how frightened they might have been or how unfairly they thought they were treated. As I said, often people find themselves, when they're young, just having to 'go along with things', especially if the person causing the problem was an authority figure or bigger than them, as in the school bully (who happens to be built like a tank).

In the classroom situation, they felt 'powerless' and that there was nothing they could do to change the outcome so they resigned themselves to having to just put up with whatever transpired, feeling a sense of hopelessness. This part of the process is an important one, because through doing it, the client can finally feel acknowledged and feel the scales are a little more balanced. As in, 'You may have hurt me, but I finally get to let you know how it felt, so you're aware of the consequence of your actions.'

Once the client has said what they would have said at the time, I ask them to forgive the person for what they did. People can struggle with forgiving someone else, especially if they feel that what the other person did was particularly nasty, because they feel as if that person hasn't paid for what they did and is now being 'let off the hook'. To them it's just not fair!

But by forgiving we're not 'condoning' what happened, we're 'letting it go', which is something else entirely. In reality, now, many years later, the only person this event is hurting is the client. The other person involved is probably completely unaware what effect they've had on their life. It's also beneficial to bear in mind that whatever the other person did—whether it was trivial or traumatic—was also a product of their own thoughts, feelings, belief systems and automatic behaviours established during their childhood—they too are flawed and have their own limitations just as we all do.

Often the process of forgiveness can be quite profound and liberating to the client. It's as if they're thinking, 'Thank God I don't have to keep carrying that around with me any longer. What a relief!' Often a big smile will appear on their face and they almost instantly look 'lighter' and happier. Other clients may find that forgiving someone completely, all in one go, is challenging, so we may continue to work on this aspect in later sessions and the client might also give more thought and conscious consideration to working on it between sessions.

This is the first part of 'neutralising the cause' . . . on to the next phase.

Re-Balancing

Once forgiveness has completely taken place or maybe just initiated, then it's time to 're-balance' the client . . . and, by this I mean, allow them to take back what was taken from them at the time of the event, or give back what they took on board at the time of the event. It's almost like returning them to the way they were before this event took place. For example, the bully might have given the client self-consciousness and it's as though the client has been carrying this with them ever since and has never quite been able to get rid of it. Consequently, it has affected every area of their life and made them overly aware of people looking at them and judging them. Equally, the teacher may have taken away the client's self-confidence by highlighting what they didn't do right to the class. In this case, it's as if their confidence was taken away and needs to be returned before the client can even begin to think of doing something which requires self-confidence, such as public speaking.

When I guide a client through this part of the process, I'm always mindful of keeping a positive aspect to it. If, for example, the thing they had to return to someone else was anger, it would be easy to direct that back with some animosity or ill-will after having dragged this anger around for so long and allowing it to affect their life so negatively.

This is again where the concept of 'blame' needs some defining, and the concept of 'letting go' needs highlighting. Most people I work through this process with, find that after they get to look at their 'cause' closely . . . and after the initial burst of emotion surrounding it has come and gone . . . are generally accepting in a quiet, pensive way of what has happened in the past and who appears to be to blame. Because we follow through and balance things out straight away, they feel quite 'at peace' with everything—which is entirely what we're trying to achieve. After the session, they might well go and talk it over with those involved, but generally in a more 'reflective' way than 'accusatory' way. What we don't want, is the client leaving their session feeling that they have to wreak revenge, and this is where I feel the hypnotherapist has a duty to ensure the subconscious mind is placated and has <u>unconditionally</u> 'let this go'.

So, to keep this part of the process all light-hearted and positive, and depending on the client's likes and dislikes, I tend to call it 'exchanging gifts'. The 'gift' could be something such as a box of chocolates, because it's usually a nice thing to give and receive. The other great thing about a box of chocolates is that even though it's just one box, say for example the box represents 'anger' all the individual chocolates inside the box might represent all the elements of the anger you carry around with you. You might have a chocolate in your box that represents 'guilt' because every time you get angry, guilt about your behaviour usually follows. There might be one that represents 'feelings of not being good enough' because that's how you feel when you can't seem to control your anger when others don't appear to have a problem. Sometimes you can appeal to the subconscious mind to identify its own chocolates that need to be returned to the other person to make things 'balanced' again.

The event or 'cause' that we discover, of course, determines what gifts are exchanged. I might, in our schoolroom scenario, get a sense that you are now carrying around a sense of panic and fear about this whole self-confidence issue and especially standing up in front of people and speaking. So I would guide you through giving back a symbolic red flashing light to the teacher and/or bully, since they caused you to be on 'red alert' from that point onwards. If, as in another example, someone experienced a childhood where they continually felt guilty even when they really had no reason to be, over the years they might have accumulated so much emotion that it had become a weighty problem. If this is the case, I might get them to imagine themselves off-loading a heavy rucksack containing all that guilt that they've been lugging around with them and giving it back to the person who initiated it. Basically, it is about identifying the elements that have been gained or lost because of the experience or event and putting it all back the way it was before . . . aahhh . . . balance. ☺

Breaking Connections

Through certain experiences and events, and then because of the ensuing habit that has formed or connection to somebody or some 'thing' that has been made, some people may need to break a connection with something. This connection can play a part in habits and addictions, whether it be alcohol, drugs, chocolate or even a relationship.

Our subconscious mind forms connections with things all the time, and the more something is repeated, whether it be mentally or physically, the stronger that connection becomes . . . sometimes to the point where it becomes a massive focus in someone's life and something they can't do without. In our school room scenario, maybe you would have formed a connection between the act of standing up to speak in front of people and the immediate physical reaction of your throat closing up.

Breaking a connection is again carried out by directing the client to firstly visualise the connection in some way. If what we're trying to break is a connection to alcohol, then I might ask the client to imagine a visible link between themselves and their usual drink—say a bottle of wine. This way, they can finally look at and acknowledge its existence and strength, and realise why it's been so hard a link to break. I will ask them to break that connection, sometimes I might describe how to do it, at other times I might allow them to visualise it in a way that they feel comfortable with, whether it be cutting it with scissors, or using a laser. I love it when people come up with their own scenarios because having that extra personal input can contribute to profound results.

One of the things I'm mindful of throughout all parts of this process, is that if you take something away, you leave a void. Voids aren't good . . . voids have to be filled . . . so it's important to ensure it's filled with something positive and of our 'conscious' choosing rather than allowing the subconscious mind to select something—with all its *'non-logic'*. After all, it could conjure up something equally as undesirable as what we just cleared, although it's more likely to just slip back into what it's always done because that's all it knows.

Again, to our schoolroom scenario . . . having cut the connection between standing up to speak in front of people and the throat closing up, we need to initiate the formation of a new connection.

So, I'd guide the client to see themselves standing up to speak and immediately being aware of the breath going in and out of their body unobstructed . . . with the airways nice and clear. To help further, I might even install a 'trigger' that the client can consciously initiate in their day-to-day life—one that the subconscious will recognise and act on. I might say: *'On standing up to speak, you'll take two long, slow, deep breaths. On those two breaths, when you breathe in, you'll imagine relaxation entering the airways, calming and relaxing all the muscles in the throat. On breathing out you will imagine letting go of any tension you might be holding on to in the physical body. This is now the cue to the subconscious mind to initiate the ability to be calm on standing up and speaking to an audience.'*

Let's take another common example . . . if we were breaking a connection to cigarettes, we might immediately form a new connection to water and embellish all the wonderful benefits the client will enjoy when drinking it. In so doing, we are giving the subconscious a reason to get excited about this wonderful new thing called water, a drink that is going to give the calm and relaxing feelings of satisfaction the cigarettes used to give. Each time the client drinks the water in the future, it will strengthen this connection that we've started and make it stronger. I would then advise the client to actively and consciously drink lots of water throughout their day. Again, the conscious effort can make a vast difference to the success of their therapy . . . because if they don't even bother carrying a bottle of water around with them, then when they do get the urge to drink it, they won't be able to, and the connection isn't strengthened.

Fading Out The Memory

This is an essential part of the neutralising process. The subconscious is <u>so</u> focused on the long-held memory, it's as though it's currently placed right at the forefront of its awareness, so although that classroom incident happened years ago, the subconscious mind is carrying on like it happened yesterday. As such, it's standing on red alert ready to save you from all the terrible and tragic things that can befall a person when standing up in front of other people and speaking.

So, to start the process of fading out this memory, I'll ask the client to imagine they're actually watching this event on a movie screen. I'll get them to notice how big it is, how loud it is, how colourful it is and how intense it feels watching it. This effectively shows how they see it today in the subconscious mind . . . but it's time to take charge of this projector and turn this movie off. It's good to make this a gradual process rather than just asking them to go up and pull the plug, because that can seem too sudden.

Firstly, again using the imagination as the key, I'll ask the client to locate the sound switch on the control panel, then while continuing to look at the screen, flick the switch to the 'off' position now encouraging positive feelings at seeing the movie with no sound. By doing this, it's lost some of its impact and I ask them to notice how much better that feels.

It's then time to change the movie from bold technicolour to black and white by flicking another switch, again noticing that the movie seems a lot less intense being just in different shades of grey . . . we all know that a black and white movie looks a little 'flat' compared to a colour one. Again I ask them to notice how much better they feel now that the movie has lost a lot more of its intensity.

Then I'll ask them to play with the focus dial and, as they do that, watch the screen to notice the images starting to go fuzzy around the edges, and then a little blurry, so they can't quite make out all the individual shapes. I encourage continuing to move the dial in this way until they can't see the picture at all . . . it's off the screen. 'How good does that feel?' What a *relief!*

But don't forget, since we've just taken something away, we have to replace it quickly with something positive. So I'll ask the client to put on a new movie of themselves, maybe projected forward by a few days, weeks or months, doing exactly what it is they want to achieve, i.e. standing in front of a roomful of people, calmly delivering a confident speech. Again, we're selling 'the benefits' to the subconscious mind so that it's willing to making the effort to change.

Separating The Child From The Adult

As a result of certain childhood experiences, a client can find themself feeling very childlike when they experience similar situations as an adult. Visiting parents would almost certainly trigger the effect of feeling as if they were shrinking down to the age of a seven year old child upon walking through the door of the parental home. This effect can ripple outwards to reach other areas of life too. If, for example, the client's mum was a perfectionist and therefore quite critical of their endeavours as a child, then the client might find themself in their adult life suddenly feeling very childlike and unable to cope when, say, their boss criticised them at work. Their automatic reaction to the criticism would have them doing *exactly* what they did as a child—quickly fleeing so that nobody could see how upset they were from feeling judged.

If I see this is as being a problem the client is carrying around with them, I would help them re-frame this mindset by asking them to imagine that the child inside, is actually stepping out of them to stand by their side. Here the subconscious can acknowledge that they are now an adult, whilst at the same time taking into consideration the child they once were.

This can also have the added effect that the client, as an adult, can now be the one to help the child. The adult is fully aware what the child needs, whether it be protection, love or encouragement, and as such, can imagine themself giving the child exactly that. As their 'child self' receives this help, (possibly for the first time ever), the positive effects will flow through to the adult self, thereby bringing about a new sense of balance.

This visualisation helps the client in their daily life by allowing them to be mindful of how their 'child self' would usually have felt compelled to react in a certain situation, that would differ from how their 'adult self' would *prefer* to react. This awareness can be enough to have them stop, think, and then *choose* to respond in the 'adult' way.

Grey-Scale

The circumstances of 'the cause', determines the techniques I use to neutralise it, and one such technique I find myself doing quite regularly is what I call the 'grey scale'. Many people's issues occur when they only see things as 'black and white'. For example, those people who struggle with getting things done because they have a perfectionist's viewpoint, believe that if they can't do something perfectly, then they won't do it at all . . . it's either 100% perfect, or it's absolute rubbish! Those who think this way often procrastinate to the point of not even starting things . . . or if they see that once they have started it they aren't doing it perfectly, they'll stop without finishing the project. All because the subconscious will consider anything that the client attempts to do as 'only' success or 'only' failure, i.e. perfection = success, but *everything* less than perfection = failure. So our task here is to allow the subconscious mind to accept that not everything is 'black or white' and that there are many other possibilities that lie between these two extremes.

When helping people with perfectionist tendencies, I'll ask them to imagine they're standing in front of a white wall, and at one end on the floor is a pot of black paint with a paintbrush in it, and at the other end is a pot of white paint with a paint brush in. The white represents 'doing something perfectly' and the black represents 'failing at something'. I then ask them to paint a vertical stripe of black paint at one end, and a stripe of white at the other, and then to start painting shades of grey by mixing the black and white, trying to create as many shades of grey as they can between the two extremes. Having done this, I ask the subconscious mind to notice all these new shades of grey and recognise that they represent all the different scenarios in-between success and failure. This way the client can start to accept that its OK to 'have a go' at something even if it's not perfect—it might just be *fun* and have nothing to do with whether they are any good at it or not.

Allowing a new concept into the subconscious in a subtle way like this, is more likely to be accepted because it seems non-threatening.

The Perfect Statue

If, as a result of our schoolroom scenario, someone is suffering from low self-esteem or a lack of self-confidence, then I might get them to build a perfect image of themself standing tall and strong, dressed in the sort of clothes they know would make them feel confident.

I might ask them to be aware of their inner self and liken this to the workings of a computer. With the client as the computer programmer, I ask them to imagine deleting any internal software that's no longer needed i.e. the one that makes them blush every time they stand up in front of a roomful of people. Then, remembering if we take something away we have to replace it quickly with something else, I'll ask them to imagine themself installing new software, perhaps one that allows them to find all the right words at the right time and lets them flow effortlessly out of their mouth.

I might then ask them to imagine merging with this image of themself . . . adopting all the positive qualities that it contains.

It's amazing what can be achieved simply because 'the subconscious mind doesn't know the difference between imagination and reality'. If the client is imagining all the things I'm telling them to, the subconscious thinks it's real and accepts it as such. This is how change can occur!

Now all we need to do is 'cement' all of this into the subconscious mind with more positive suggestion and lots and lots of repetition!

CHAPTER 11

RE-PROGRAMMING

This part of the process is what I'd call the 'mainstay' of any hypnotherapist's work. It may well be what many hypnotherapists focus on when they don't endeavour to find 'the cause', although hopefully awareness is growing as more and more research is showing the benefits of finding it.

So, by this point the subconscious mind has been through quite an upheaval. It's been woken up to the fact that there's a huge problem and it knows that means it will have to make some changes, and that's big stuff because essentially it's been reacting the same way since childhood.

Our priority, therefore, is to present the idea of change in a positive way so that it's more likely to be accepted by the subconscious. Change to the subconscious can seem too difficult and maybe even threatening because it views what it doesn't know as being scary. As such, we can't always be obvious about it, but instead, might have to use tactics that mean it's delivered more subtly . . . even to the point of being hidden. Uplifting stories relayed as happening to other people, and metaphors that mean you can say what you want without actually saying it can be particularly effective methods of infiltrating positive change into the subconscious.

As I'm sure you've gathered from reading this book so far, each and every person has been created by the same process—through the culmination of childhood experiences. However, *not one* person on this planet has had exactly the same childhood experiences as any another, which makes each person unique. So, a big part of a hypnotherapist's work is tailoring their re-programming to individually suit the person in the chair, and having found 'the cause' means we can be *specific* how we do this.

If a hypnotherapist tried to use the 'one fits all' approach, they would soon realise that what works for one client, may not work for another, simply because it will depend on the client's unique subconscious view of life.

As people learn by repetition, a hypnotherapist will deliver the new positive suggestions many times, preferably over a few sessions if given the opportunity. Remember that because the subconscious doesn't know the difference between reality and imagination, the hypnotherapist can encourage the imagination to rehearse the desired changes over and over so that by the time the client enacts it in real life, the subconscious is used to it, and just adopts the behaviour automatically and easily.

This is also where I feel that finding 'the cause' makes a significant difference to whether a new behaviour gets accepted by the subconscious mind, or doesn't. After all, if we're continually trying to tell it to do something different, but all it can focus on is the fear of 'the cause', this fear is more than likely to override any new suggestions. While neutralising 'the cause' first, and any fear that goes with it, means that the new positive suggestions stand a greater chance of being accepted and incorporated into the subconscious mind, and becoming part of the client's new positive behaviour pattern.

Selling It To The Subconscious

One of the things hypnotherapists are continually looking for is ingenious ways to get around any barriers the subconscious may put up. Is there a particular way of saying something? Can they cleverly hide their message so the subconscious 'gets it' but doesn't feel threatened at the same time? Would telling it that someone else had a similar problem and solved it in a certain way be a better approach?

I find that most issues are multi-faceted and therefore the most effective way to approach the positive suggestion is from different angles. This is true not only in the language I use, and whether I directly address the subconscious or hide the message a little by telling a story, or focus on visualisations of outcomes, but I also find that talking about the different aspects of the change itself can also be helpful.

For example, if I'm helping someone with weight management issues, I won't *just* talk about how they should eat from now on. But first, I might talk to them about creating a foundation of self-esteem as a base on which to build everything, and then I might address the subconscious about helping the client to generally think more positively, followed by self-confidence suggestions. Then I'll follow with actual direct suggestions, on how the subconscious will now automatically eat, i.e. regular healthy meals and lots of water, not eating when bored or eating for comfort. This all-round approach appears to encourage a more thorough, beneficial change.

Rehearsing The Change

Rehearsing the changes and the end result is a useful and effective method of making changes within the subconscious. For our classroom scenario, I might ask the client to imagine and rehearse their next boardroom presentation whilst constantly prompting them and reminding them throughout the rehearsal that they are calm, relaxed and the words are flowing. The rush of adrenalin they're feeling is best used in a positive way to deliver their speech with enthusiasm, therefore nervousness is something positive, instead of negative.

We have already introduced this 'rehearsing' concept previously in our work together when encouraging the subconscious to see both the reason for change and introducing *how* to change. But here, whilst focusing on the subconscious re-programming and re-learning part of the work, we'll repeat this *many* times to allow the subconscious to become completely familiar with this new way of doing things. So much so, that when it happens in real life, the subconscious thinks it's carried it out numerous times already, and now finds it to be natural and not at all scary. It's a bit like, 'Oh yes, we're doing this again—no worries. We've done it *lots* of times before . . . Cool!'

The Importance Of Relaxation

Deep relaxation is something that's often experienced during hypnosis. I believe that throughout our lives, most people rarely practice the art of relaxation. Yet when they need it because something stressful is going on, they find themselves desperately trying to produce it 'on demand'. The chances of this happening of course are virtually nil, which only adds to their worry as they then get anxious about not being able to calm themselves when they need to . . . again, another merry-go-round of worry.

For a client experiencing hypnosis, being relaxed is therefore another way of teaching their subconscious *how* to be relaxed, allowing the 'relaxation' to become a tool in itself. So, I would take the opportunity to point out that relaxation is *certainly* better than feeling anxious and stressed, therefore encouraging the subconscious to choose to be calm and relaxed under future situations where it would previously have triggered an anxious response.

Added to just asking the subconscious mind to recognise the beneficial state of relaxation, a post-hypnotic 'trigger' can be installed which the client initiates in their day-to-day life when they feel they need to calm themselves. The subconscious mind will then recognise this trigger and follow through with inducing the state of relaxation. The trigger could be as simple as the client taking two nice, long deep breaths, or squeezing their thumb and finger together, or even saying 'Relax' three times. A trigger can become a very reliable tool for the client to use when they need extra help.

Is It Mind Control?

The re-programming part of the hypnotherapy process is often what clients worry about the most for fear of it being 'mind control'. Concerns include: 'What if the hypnotherapist makes me do something I don't want to do?' 'What if the hypnotherapist persuades me to give them my bank account number and steals all my money and I don't know anything about it!'

First of all, hypnotherapists are here to help, they are therapists— admittedly in any occupation there are unscrupulous people which is why I have stressed the importance of finding a registered hypnotherapist—and secondly, your subconscious mind is your protector, it's constantly on guard for such things. I always explain to clients that if they felt compelled to stop the session and get up and walk out, they could do so quite easily—and they could. Remember, nine times out of ten, there is still an element of a client's conscious logical, mind in attendance.

Repetition, Repetition, Repetition . . .

There are many things that can be achieved during the re-programming part of the therapy and ultimately this is what the client came for—to train themselves to do something differently to what they were doing before. The level of repetition required to achieve this change, differs from client to client.

This part of the process is now likely to be successful because of the work we've already done together, because having found and neutralised 'the cause' we're not fighting against years of deep-seated emotional barriers that would have previously blocked the positive suggestions from being accepted. Now change is likely to be achieved.

Even though I don't 'focus' on re-programming until the third session, I have already woven it into the first two sessions. I've planted the seeds of change by firstly presenting the benefits of change to the subconscious, I continue with the concentrated positive re-programming at the end of the second session, and then the third session and any further reinforcement sessions required, comprising of <u>lots</u> of repetitive positive suggestion. Repeatedly telling the client to do something of benefit, and planting this information *exactly* where it's needed, contributes greatly to *actually* effecting change since repetition is how we humans learn.

Taking Back Control Of Your Thoughts

Thought → Feeling → Response/Action

This is the process that you, as a human being, goes through when something happens around you or to you. You have a thought about it, this triggers a feeling within you and then you enact your automatic response and/or action from the subconscious mind.

There are many books available about the 'Law of Attraction' and how we can use it to improve our lives by focussing on better thoughts. This little equation, therefore, I believe, essentially contributes to how we work with the law of attraction in our daily lives. <u>Everything</u> starts from your thoughts and as the subconscious doesn't know the difference between reality and imagination, then as far as it's concerned your thoughts *are* your reality and it will respond accordingly.

'What you focus on becomes your reality'.

The problem we have is that with all our good intentions after reading a book on thinking better thoughts and getting all fired up to change our lives by changing our thoughts, try as we might, maintaining the consistency that's needed, seems impossible. Why? Because our thoughts tend to get hijacked easily by what's happening to us during our day and by what other people are doing and saying around us.

So, apart from planting positive suggestions within the subconscious mind about switching to better, more positive thoughts quickly and easily, I also give clients some practical, conscious things to do to help them take control of their thought patterns. None of these things are new or ground-breaking and there are many books outlining the same types of things, but I'm including them here because I know they work . . . and I know, because I did them all myself and they changed my life profoundly. It did take consistency and, therefore, time, but the monumental change in my day-to-day thoughts compared to a few years earlier was life-changing for me.

When we get caught up in the negativity going on around us, we tend to 'give in' to it too easily . . . 'it' happens, 'it' makes us feel bad, 'it's in control of our emotions and so 'it' determines whether we have a good or a bad day. Of course, things will always happen around us, but it's our *choice* whether we let these things 'control' our happiness or not.

Years ago, I started to realise that it was time to balance the scales in my life. I was generally caught up in day-to-day negative thoughts that were making my life miserable. So, after reading some inspiring 'pick-me-up' kind of books, I decided that if something happened in my day to make me feel bad, then I'd go and do something that made me feel good. It needed to be something easy, cheap, and not time-consuming or require too much effort, otherwise I just wouldn't have the time or money to do it, and would no doubt choose not to do it . . . and so would remain unhappy.

I LOVE coffee! So what I started to do was make more of a 'big deal' about my coffee moments. Rather than drinking it mindlessly, as I often did without even registering that I was doing something I enjoyed, I decided to make my coffee moments an uplifting break in my day. ☺

It didn't cost much, and it didn't take much time. I focused on buying a tasty coffee, and savouring every mouthful and tuning into how delicious every mouthful was. Occasionally, if I had time I'd go somewhere scenic to drink it or buy a magazine and read it, savouring the moment even more so. In time I realised that I was starting to remind myself of how it felt to be happy about something. I looked forward to these moments of happiness and ultimately realised, as I was doing this, that I was **actually in control of my happiness**. I could choose to bring it into any part of my day—and I especially did so if something horrible had happened earlier.

As time went by, I thought of a few other similar things that I could bring into my day to have some 'happy' time, and before long I realised that I was spending much of my day feeling good. *I liked feeling good!* It helped me to enjoy my days even when I didn't have something 'big' to look forward to.

Throughout our lives we tend to set future goals, and look forward to achieving them. We might also be focused on attending future events that we know we'll enjoy, whether it be a holiday in six months-time, or a big party in three months-time. We also have those long-term goals where we find ourselves saying—'It'll all be OK when I pay my house off and don't have a mortgage anymore—*then I'll be happy!*' But we become *so* focused on those long-distance goals that we don't find any enjoyment during the bit in-between now and then. We trundle along and just 'get on with life' and only save happiness for the 'big' things. But, the cliché I'm sure you've heard many times before is *so* true:

'Life is a journey, not a destination.'

We are always overly focused on the destination—the goal—so much so that the journey towards the goal often becomes unimportant and mundane. We seem to just 'endure' our day-to-day life, only managing to muster up enjoyment from the odd 'big event' that pops up to interrupt the monotony.

So for me, this little easy-to-do exercise of purposefully, consciously and actively ensuring I brought enjoyment into my day helped me immensely. The great thing about it was that it was *so* easy to start. When we think about making the shift from being generally unhappy to achieving happiness, all we can see is that our goal is so far away from where we are now, that it's unreachable, and that the chasm in between seems too big and daunting to justify the effort. So we try for a while, but give up very quickly when we feel we haven't made enough progress. This coffee exercise, however, makes it easy and do-able straight away—*today!*

Practical exercises are a great way to promote change for clients. So, another little exercise I encourage people to do, especially those who are struggling with self-confidence issues or who are not feeling good enough in some way, is to write a list of everything they've achieved in their life that they're proud of . . . their innate qualities that they feel good about and the general things about themselves that they like. Once they have started the list, they can then add to it every day. Generally, when people are feeling down, one of the first things they do is berate themselves, not finding a kind word to say and then automatically focusing on all their 'bad bits'.

However, when clients write their positive thoughts down on paper, those thoughts suddenly become tangible and part of their reality, as opposed to 'things' just swimming aimlessly around in their head that they conveniently forget when they need them the most. Seeing a list of their good qualities validates them as 'worthy' and, each day, as they add to their list, it helps them to shift their thoughts from negative to positive more of the time, and helps them learn to think about themselves differently. The things on their list don't have to be monumental as in, 'I achieved a bachelor's degree in science', the little things are just as important. 'I gave up my seat on the bus to someone' or 'I responded calmly today when normally I would have got angry', are equally worthy.

This list is just another active way for clients to start shifting their focus onto feeling more positive. It's also a way of planning ahead for the challenging times. If they're having a particularly bad day and can't think of anything positive, and can't get out of their 'pit of despair' . . . they can read their list—prove to themselves that things aren't always bad and that they're not always negative.

I also encourage people to daydream about the positive things that we've programmed into their subconscious. It fuels the whole process, and just doing this can mean propelling the client from having 'OK' results to having 'fantastic' results.

Having been through my own experiments with my thoughts and feelings, I do feel as if I've come through a mist of confusion, emerging on the other side into clarity, where I truly understand that I *do* get to choose my own happiness.

Much of what we think 'now' is projected into the future—we do, of course, think about what has happened in the past, but only in as much as, 'now that's happened, this or that *could* happen, or that person might now think *this* about me'. Whether it's consistent worry or just negative feelings, we always think about what *will* happen.

I often say to people who are caught up in consistently negative or worrying thoughts:

> *The things that you're getting all worked up or feeling*
> *down about, may or may not happen, but your worrying*
> *will not actually have any bearing on the outcome.*
> *Many things happen or don't happen regardless of*
> *whether you worry about them. In fact, you could*
> *spend a long time getting upset and focusing on all*
> *the worst possible scenarios and yet <u>none</u> of them may*
> *actually eventuate . . . making all that upset pointless.*

These thoughts of the future do serve a purpose, of course, because we need to know what we're doing next. We usually have to plan ahead, be ready 'just in case', and use past knowledge to make sure we're prepared, sometimes to avert disasters . . . but there's a difference between being generally mindful in a positive way, and getting so caught up in all the negativity of this process that it becomes all-consuming.

These little simple-to-do exercises are a good starting point to easily and actively interrupt the habit of thinking negatively and if done often enough, there will be a positive shift to generally better thoughts. In effect this will become your new habit—and a very welcome one.

CHAPTER 12

MAINTENANCE

G enerally, we know if someone went to a hypnotherapist—indeed, any therapist—they would hope to be 'fixed' permanently by the end of their therapy. With hypnotherapy though, I think the expectation is even greater—that change will be 'totally and forever'.

I've come to realise, that although permanent change is always both the therapist's and the client's ultimate goal, the problem, is that life is ever-changing in itself and nobody knows what will come their way to give them a bit of a 'wobble' in the future.

So, I view the *'permanence'* of change a little bit differently from the 'totally and forever' concept as mentioned above. I like to think the changes I help a client achieve, mean their everyday life is *generally* the way they'd like it to be (whether for them that is to be anxiety-free, to exercise more or to have more confidence to actually do the things they want to do). However, sometimes their life could deliver something unexpected, profoundly life-changing or tragic. When this happens, it would be natural for them to have a bigger, negative reaction—one that upsets their newly-acquired balance they've achieved from hypnotherapy. It's also natural that the subconscious would choose its old and more familiar way of reacting when it feels under sudden or excessive pressure.

'The cause' that we've neutralised can never be *completely* erased—the subconscious records everything that has ever happened to someone. We've managed to 're-frame' it and file it deep down in the archives, but if something comes along that's big enough, then chances are it will come into play and the client might well find they experience some of the old symptoms. When this happens, the client may well get despondent, because at the first hint of those familiar symptoms, they assume that all their anxiety has come back with full force and that hypnotherapy didn't work after all. They might even find themselves saying something like, *'I knew it was too good to last!'*

Realistic expectation is key here. I *always* tell my clients to come back for some top-up sessions at the first sign of old ways, that way we can address it quickly and remind the subconscious of the new behaviours that we've taught it. Remember, it's just panicking a bit and acting out of fear.

As indicated above, clients may have a wobble and therefore come back for more hypnotherapy, usually because something fairly 'big' or unexpected has happened in their life, maybe their relationship with their partner has ended, they lost their job or they developed an illness. There are some clients, however, who just slide slowly back to old habits and they simply need more 'learning' until the subconscious really does 'get it', and starts to adopt the changes as the new 'usual' way of doing things.

I also have some clients who come back regularly for ongoing hypnotherapy . . . for no particular reason, other than they understand how well hypnotherapy works for them. It keeps them 'in line' and 'on course' with what they want to achieve. It might just be regular 'top-ups' of self-confidence to keep the momentum going, or regular deep relaxation to remind the subconscious mind how beneficial relaxation is, so that it continues to choose it in their day-to-day lives.

I suppose you could liken hypnotherapy maintenance to having your car serviced . . . you know that when your car is first on the road it's not going to get you through your daily life safely and smoothly if it's not maintained along the way. Your car will experience harsh weather, general mechanical wear and tear, bumpy roads and the odd pothole to give it a real jolt now and then. However, you know that a regular service will keep your car in good working order, reliably getting you from A to B as you need it to. Hypnotherapy is the same and can be thought of as the 'Service for your Mind'.

PART 3

SOME THINGS YOU MIGHT RECOGNISE . . . COMMON ISSUES, TRAITS AND GENERAL OBSERVATIONS

CHAPTER 13

WE ARE ALL COMPLETELY UNIQUE IN A SIMILAR WAY

So—what's out there that's causing so much upheaval in our lives? Although the circumstances of anyone's 'cause' of their issue is totally unique, it sets in motion a range of emotional responses, automatic behaviours and belief systems that then become the problem or issue, that then usually gets a generic 'label' stamped on it.

This part of the book is about the things I've come to notice through working with hundreds and hundreds of clients . . . because I've found that there are similar *types* of causes that pop up time and time again, as well as similar *types* of issues that they can ignite in people. So, as much as we are unique, we are also so similar and connected to each other in many ways. Despite this, clients usually feel totally on their own in their angst, to the point of not being able to talk to anyone else. Hopefully, this section of the book will help those who feel as if they're perceived differences are causing problems in their life, because if the issue is mentioned here, then it's because many people who have sat in my chair have experienced it. So, take heart from reading the following pages and think how many other people out in the world will also be going through something similar to you.

As humans, we naturally want to 'belong' and fit in with those around us. In fact, this is an issue in itself and quite widespread as the awareness of wanting to 'belong' is an integral part of growing up for us all. This aspect is especially true of people with anxiety. The symptoms of the anxiety seem so irrational that most people assume they must be the only ones suffering from it, and they become too embarrassed to admit to other people what they're experiencing for fear of ridicule. That fear of ridicule, and more specifically 'being judged', seems to be one of <u>the</u> biggest issues we humans struggle with.

Being judged is the 'roof' under which everything else is housed. It is, in my mind, *the* most common element behind so many issues, yet is so complicated and all-encompassing that it can be broken down into sub categories. I only realised as I was writing this section of the book—just how many of the elements that come up repeatedly for clients as types of 'causes', are simply an aspect of the *awareness of being judged*.

Waves Of Issues

Another interesting observation I have made throughout my work as a hypnotherapist is what I call 'waves of issues'. I'll explain what I mean by this, but I have absolutely no idea what it is or why it happens! (If anyone out there knows, please put me out of my misery!)

It is sometimes bizarre how, within a short space of time, I'll have an influx of clients with the same issue. I may not see a client for 'nail biting' in six months, and then suddenly I have 4 all at once. Before I'd never even dealt with someone with Trichotillomania (I'd never even heard of it) then, two clients within the space of a month come to see me for it—with no obvious relationship connection between them.

I often have clients with different presenting issues, i.e. one with anxiety and the other with weight management, but there will be an odd 'cause' component that's identical. When I have repetitions like this, it usually wakens my mind up to something going on that I hadn't considered. These realisations can be helpful and insightful, giving me a new awareness that I can implement in helping not only those clients, but also future clients. In fact, this awareness has allowed me to put together this part of the book by highlighting connections, coincidences and things that come up again and again.

I'd like to emphasise here, yet again, that we are all unique. One type of cause, i.e. our classroom scenario can initiate any number of issues depending on the client's collective life's experiences up to that point. So in one client this experience may initiate a heightened fear of being judged; in another client, it might set off a fear of rejection; in someone else, it could ignite a fear of authority figures; in another, it could spark off an awareness of a fear of failure—the outcomes are endless.

As I am not a psychologist or counsellor, this book is not based on taught theories of human behaviour. However, my system of working, which involves detailed conscious and subconscious information-gathering has allowed me to piece together all the information in this book—particularly this section. It is purely a 'collection' of my observations of clients. Marrying together information I glean from them at the beginning of their therapy by finding out exactly how they see the world; what words they use to describe their world and the words they use to describe themselves, the things they repeat but in different contexts and then putting this together with what they say during their regression.

I often discuss my theories with the psychologists and counsellors I work alongside at my therapy centre, (in fact, we often work *together* with clients to help them on all levels). I've mentioned to them my observation about 'waves of issues' and it seems this runs through much of their world too. We've also ascertained that we are collectively busy or collectively quiet . . . and not just because its school holidays, or Christmas, or Easter, or because of the GFC, but just *because!*

The following pages include some, but not all 'labelled' issues I have worked with, there would be way too many to include in one book. My observations also do not include the entirety of any one issue as again each one would be a book in itself and overly complicated, and the very point of *this* particular book is to keep it simple.

The notes that I've made for each issue are those which I've found to be noticeably prominent and/or interesting to me and by making you aware of them I hope they will be helpful to you too.

Along with 'real' issues, are general observations that I've endeavoured to make up a label for, because they have cropped up enough times to make them stand out in some way as having meaning, or some possible bearing on human behaviour . . . even if I'm not entirely sure why.

So, here goes . . .

CHAPTER 14

GOING AGAINST YOUR BELIEF SYSTEM

I would like to start by outlining the importance of 'the' belief system . . . I feel this will help you, the reader, have an even greater understanding of why some seemingly 'small' issues can actually end up being huge, purely because a person is trying to *oppose* their own deep-rooted belief system.

A belief system is created to help us make sense of the world around us, and specifically the world around us **at the time when we were growing up**. Its purpose is to help us to deal with our environment and to know what to expect and therefore, how to react to get through life safely. The problem, however, is that as we grow up, our world tends to change as we go to school, make new friends, move house, get a job, have relationships, etc . . . and so our belief system is tested time and again as we progress through life.

Also, as we get older and broaden our horizons, we see what else is going on in the world around us, things that maybe we haven't experienced before, but would quite like to. Consciously these experiences look good, others seem to be enjoying them . . . but the real angst occurs when what we aspire to does <u>not</u> match our old childhood belief system—and the more opposing of it that it is, the more turmoil, and often anxiety, that can result from trying to achieve it.

People struggle with relationships when, for example, they recognise that they like the idea of family life . . . being married and filling a house full of love and laughter as they've noticed others doing. But this concept might be so far removed from their own childhood experience . . . which created their belief system that 'love wasn't expressed', or didn't even appear to exist . . . that making the leap from one extreme to the other, is unlikely to be a successful one, while also causing huge amounts of inner conflict.

Our subconscious mind operates around what it knows, and even if we're consciously aware of a belief system that might seem a negative one to have to carry around with us, the subconscious doesn't really see it like that. It likes the fact that it's helping to keep things as they've always been . . . it likes what it knows . . . the familiarity makes it feel safe. After all, its primary role is to keep you safe.

Of course, also to be considered is the fact that many people are completely unaware of what their belief systems actually are. Then everything really does seem like a confusing, frustrating mess when all their endeavours to achieve their dreams seem continually sabotaged. In the example of trying to have a loving relationship, the self-sabotage may well come in the form of starting arguments for no apparent reason, or behaving in a way that really annoys your partner. This will obviously create unrest between you both, however, your subconscious will actually be happy with itself. It's brought the environment back to what it knows—one where little love is expressed, because your partner spends so much time not talking to you because he or she is so upset at your behaviour.

Self-belief systems can come in many different flavours . . . there are some common and wide-ranging ones, for example believing that you're a failure . . . causing you to self-sabotage all your attempts to get ahead in life. There are some that are a little more obscure, and there are those that seem 'precise' . . . for example, believing that if you don't tap your head ten times before you exit a room then someone around you will be harmed, which, of course, is a typical Obsessive Compulsive Disorder trait.

When you truly recognise that these belief systems have a profound and far-reaching impact on your everyday life, by keeping you stuck in old behaviour patterns, or feeling so 'out of control', then it also stands to reason that if you can, through hypnotic regression, identify them and change them to something more positive, then the results can be truly life-changing.

People can, as they go about their everyday lives, armed with the knowledge of what's been bubbling away under the surface for so long, actually be mindful of what they are doing and why, and this can then consciously back-up the subconscious changes we're asking to be made.

Subconscious + conscious teamwork = positive change

CHAPTER 15

THE FEAR OF
BEING JUDGED

It seems to me that absolutely _everyone_ has a degree of this awareness. In fact, when you think about it, it's an essential part of us as individual beings living within a society. How would society even exist if we didn't have it within us? For society to actually work it's important that we care whether we act in an acceptable way in other people's eyes.

It's important that we're mindful of whether others see us as generous, loving, conscientious and hard-working, considerate or intelligent . . . and we are equally concerned that people _don't_ see us as being selfish, uncaring, cruel, petty, big-headed, stupid or incapable . . . the list goes on. You can imagine therefore, with this many '_do's_' and '_don'ts_' that society requires of us, that it's no wonder we're all concerned about what others judge us 'to be' or 'not to be'.

Yes, that is the question that we're continually asking ourselves— and we're often our own harshest critic when we come up with an answer. Not that we usually arrive at it by looking at everything clearly and weighing up all the facts. Instead, we usually find our answer by looking at everything through our glasses with the 'perception of the facts filter' stuck on the lenses (which is, of course, dependent on one's life's experiences). So our *perception* of how we think others see us is often different from the *reality* of how others *actually* see us.

Much of the time people are generally unaware that this concept of 'being judged' is bubbling away under the surface, despite many of the issues it causes seeming quite irrational, and this is especially true of anxiety. Anxiety just seems completely *nuts* to the people who experience it, they think and do things that make no sense at all, yet they seem to have no control over them.

It's a lot more disconcerting for a client when they fear something that they can't identify. For example, a person might have an underlying awareness of being judged if they stood up in front of a roomful of strangers to introduce themselves, but outwardly, they might be totally at a loss as to why they feel this sense of panic, when logically they know that standing up and saying 'My name is Sam,' won't *actually* hurt them in any way. In comparison, having a fear of something tangible, such as a snake, is more acceptable, because they know logically, that yes, that snake could actually bite them and cause them to be sick.

However, when I take clients back to the cause of their anxiety, and they re-connect with the incident that initiated it, they can straight away feel a sense of calmness *just* from having identified it . . . '*Thank God—there is a reason for my behaviour!*'

***We all have experiences in our younger years that
kick-start this awareness of having a place in society
and that <u>others are watching what we're doing!</u>***

If you knew that standing up in class reading out loud and stumbling on your words so that the whole class laughs was an important part of your history, you could no doubt answer your question, 'Why don't I like to stand up in front of others and talk?' . . .

Because your subconscious is expecting everyone in the audience to *judge you* on your ability to say the right words and they'll laugh if you don't get it right. For someone else, the answer to that question may be that the experience as a child that stood out for them, was that their mum told them one day, 'Whatever you do, make sure you brush your hair before you go out. You can't go out looking like you've been dragged through a hedge backwards. *What will the neighbours think?*' This experience might cause their awareness in a roomful of strangers to be focused on the audience *judging* them and possibly criticising their appearance and deeming them to be 'not up to scratch'.

For the one issue, there could be many different scenarios that have firstly caused it, and then contributed to how it's played out in day-to-day life.

> *I've found it interesting to help clients discover the little things in their early years that started their issue.*

I'm sure you can see as you're reading this book, how many 'little' experiences in our lives are actually important because they highlight the things we're subconsciously focused on, but are consciously unaware of.

> *Where is our own unique focus on how we feel judged by the world—and what do we do, or not do, in response to that awareness?*

By undergoing the hypnosis process I've outlined in this book, the potential to *really* find out who you are and why you do what you do could be freeing and life-changing. How enlightening and empowering would it be to be able to truly know yourself? To make sense of who you *really* are and then *choose* how you'd like to be in the future?

To help someone neutralise the cause of this issue . . . the event that started it all . . . I would guide them through forgiving whoever said or did something to raise their heightened awareness that people can judge them and how uncomfortable it can feel. I then might ask the client to imagine giving back the sense of being on 'red alert' that would go off every time someone asked them to stand up and speak . . . a feeling they've carried with them since the original event. Then, as I've taken something away and left a void, I'll ask them to imagine filling that void with something positive. This is often the sense of self-confidence which was taken from them at the same time . . . because of what 'that' person did or said. So I'll ask them to imagine getting the other person to return it to them to fill the void. This new sense of self-confidence is a real foundation for them to build the changing process on, and to bring the specific things they're wanting into their lives.

Up to this point in time, this particular experience, which now sits as a memory, has been very much at the forefront of their subconscious mind, and as such has been continually reminding it of the potential to be harshly judged. To change this, I'll then guide the client through effectively fading out the scene, to make it smaller, and send it to the back of the mind where it won't be used as the trigger it's always been.

It's like re-jigging your filing system . . . you have the stuff you need and want every day on your desk in your in-tray and easily accessible, then the other less important stuff is in your office filing cabinet, so that it's locked away, but handy when you need it every now and again . . . and the things that have been dealt with but just need to be kept for tax reasons, are down in the vaults because you hardly refer to them anymore.

Then, I use repetition of the positive suggestions to direct the subconscious on what to do from then on. To teach it how the client wants to be, what they want to do and how they want to feel standing up in front of people and talking in the future. I'll also enhance this by asking the client to imagine actually being, doing and feeling all those things, rehearsing it in their mind over and over so the subconscious thinks it's already happening, and starts to adopt it as something familiar and beneficial, rather than the potential threat it saw it as being previously.

Through this process, the client has understood why they've been experiencing anxiety for so many years, neutralised the cause that has triggered it every time, and then re-learnt and accepted a new way of doing things that allows him/her to stand up and talk in front of others with no anxiety . . . and, I'm sure, a lot happier for it!

CHAPTER 16

THE FEAR OF 'NOT BELONGING'

As I've mentioned, Being Judged is the roof under which many other causes or issues sit, and Not Belonging might be one of the rooms in this house for you, or maybe just a brick in one of the walls, or perhaps the whole west wing!

When we feel as if we don't belong, it's usually because we feel someone has judged us and decided that we don't fit in in some way. Sometimes it may be that others don't allow us in, but also, *we* can decide within ourselves that we are different and can find incredible ways of being on the outside of everything, segregating ourselves even though it's not what we consciously want and don't understand why we do it.

Again, the things that might start this mindset can be trivial. Being the only person in a class who wears glasses can make you feel different, regardless of whether you decide this for yourself, recognising that no-one else is wearing them, or other kids in the class deciding to make fun of you because of it. Again, that awareness of being judged by others creeps in.

As humans, I feel it is our innate need to 'belong' to a family, to the 'gang' of friends, to society. We need to know where our place is, and that we are accepted by others. The best way for this to happen is to be as similar to the other people in the family or group of friends as we can be. Why do you think so many people take up smoking, when it's the most disgusting thing in the world to breathe in a mouthful of smoke? All you smokers out there, can you honestly say that when you had your first drag of a cigarette you thought to yourself, *'That was mighty fine. I really enjoyed the smoothness of the smoke going into my lungs. It gave me a real sense of calmness and relaxation, and I feel as if all my troubles have suddenly gone. It's wonderful stuff this tobacco!'* . . . No?

'No' is right! I'm pretty sure it was more something like this: *'What the 'bleep' was that? Oh my God, that was disgusting! How on earth am I gonna do that again without throwing up and embarrassing myself?'* Followed by cough, cough, cough. So why did you keep on doing something that is as unnatural and uncomfortable as trying to climb up a fir tree naked? Because you wanted to *'belong'* to the cool group of smokers that stood together at break time in the playground.

Going through the teenage years can *especially* have you questioning your sense of belonging, even in your own family. As you start to expand your awareness of the world and see that other people do things differently to your family, some of which you didn't even know existed before, opens up more questions and options for you than it gives answers and makes you doubt your place in the world.

Carrying a sense of 'not belonging' through-out your life can seem like a continual up-hill battle, because as you get older a few things come into play, but primarily because your conscious mind wants the exact opposite to what your subconscious mind is used to.

I mentioned before about your belief systems . . . well, let's say you grew up in a family where your parents divorced quite young and you found yourself being passed around from one family member to another, which you perceived as 'nobody wanting you'. Here you created your self-belief system of *'I don't really belong anywhere . . . nobody seems to want me'*. Now you're older, and your 'conscious' mind has started looking around at other people and decided that maybe it would be nice to get married and be part of a family, after all, everyone else seems to be doing it. But, as you start to pursue this line of thought, your subconscious is alerted and aware that belonging to a family is not congruent to its 'I don't belong' belief system. This is where self-sabotage comes along to make sure it doesn't happen . . . initiating arguments in your relationship with your partner, having an affair, constantly doing things that you know your partner doesn't like, and so on. My word, there are so many *wonderful* ways to sabotage a relationship, aren't there?

This self-belief system is particularly antagonising, since it's our natural human instinct to 'belong' and yet this belief system totally opposes it. People often find themselves in complete turmoil as they try to 'fit in' to life, with people, and at work and just about everything. The level of anxiety here can be tremendous and clients usually turn it on themselves by blaming themselves for being the ones who don't fit in, assuming there must be something wrong with them. It's almost like the world having a joke and they are just not being let in on it.

Even though the cause of 'not belonging' can be a one-off event that initiated this thought-concept, I've found that clients who suffer extreme anxiety and depression because of this self-belief system often have several incidents through their childhood years that have re-sensitised and magnified it. Alternatively, they were brought up in a family environment where they were exposed to constant reminders on a daily basis that they weren't wanted, were unappreciated or felt 'invisible'.

Apart from the usual forgiveness of whoever created this concept in the client's mind, I also make sure that we introduce the 'belonging' concept to the subconscious mind. Whilst they are in hypnosis, and the subconscious is watching and learning how to 'be' I'll ask them to visualise themselves interacting with the environment they wish to belong to, whether it be their own family, their work environment, or hanging out with their social group. Throughout our sessions, I'll get them to rehearse this experience again and again, so that the subconscious mind can see how good it feels, how beneficial it is, and that it's enjoyable and not at all scary.

When the subconscious mind is familiar with something and accepts it as reality even whilst in hypnosis (remember, it doesn't know that I'm just asking the client to imagine it, it thinks that because they're thinking it, it's really happening), then when it comes to that situation happening in real life, the fear has subsided. As far as it's concerned, this new experience has already successfully happened many times (even though it's only been through use of imagination).

CHAPTER 17

I'M NOT
GOOD ENOUGH

This is a slightly different slant on Being Judged, because when someone feels 'not good enough', it's because they are comparing themselves with others and *always* arriving at the conclusion that they don't 'measure up' in some way.

Self-sabotaging to live up to this belief system is especially prominent, annoying and debilitating to the client because they'll usually do something subconsciously themselves to make sure they fail. Why? Because this proves to them once again, that, 'Yes, indeed, they're not good enough to achieve anything, be loved by anyone, or be valued in any way'.

Even if they actually *do* succeed at something, they rarely feel the pleasure of obtaining it, because they're almost waiting for someone to come along and say 'Ah, but it's not *really* that good, is it?' In fact, they will probably get in first and fulfil that expectation themselves by playing it down in some way. You could lavish sincere, heartfelt praise on such a person and they'd never actually believe you. They rarely get a sense of satisfaction, enjoyment or peace out of anything they do, because their overwhelming sense of 'not being good enough' clouds everything.

Another slight nuance within this issue is that a person feels as if they're not good enough in more of a, 'I'm not good enough to be *deserving*' way, so they seldom allow themselves to do anything just for themself. They do a lot for others, but if their conscious mind steps in and decides, 'you work hard, you *do* deserve to do things for yourself as well', they are more likely to justify acquiring or achieving things, if they frame it in a way that someone else reaps the benefits. For them to have something purely for themself feels almost selfish, in their mind they don't deserve it and so it's overshadowed by massive waves of guilt.

While this internal battle takes place, the turmoil can be overwhelming. Their conscious mind is involved in the equation and strives to obtain things, and wishes to be fully recognised for them, but their subconscious mind might feel completely unworthy of say, getting a new promotion at work . . . to the point of feeling guilty. The client might feel 'out of their depth' and assume that everyone thinks they're not actually capable of doing the new job. They might feel they don't really deserve to be there at all and so feel guilty they've even been promoted, although in their reasoning, they probably only got the job because nobody else wanted it. Lots of these little conversations are going on every moment of every day, each fuelling the anxiety and the self-doubt.

Yet these overwhelming feelings of self-doubt always occur because of somebody else! One person who had an opinion about them, who judged and compared them, and decided that they weren't good enough in some way, and that sparked the self-doubt. The client might have sparked it themselves, but only because they'd compared themselves to someone else and deemed the other person to be better in some way.

It seems to me, that when we judge ourselves, we always seem to assume that the person we're comparing ourselves with is the one who is better in some way, that they are the 'right' one, that they are the benchmark. When someone appears to judge us, we'll automatically assume that it's a negative judgement even if we don't actually know it to be so. Sometimes people just have to look in our direction and we assume they're thinking something bad about us, and, if people do actually *say* something even vaguely negative about us, then we believe them to be right. This is especially true when we're growing up or if that criticism comes from an adult, because we have an awareness that adults are right, they're to be believed and we learn from them the way the world is. We also pay attention to our peer groups because we want to fit in, so we'll believe what they say too.

The cause of 'not being good enough' is usually someone literally making a negative comment or judgement and the client then adopting that opinion as the truth, which for them became a focus that they applied to many different aspects of their life, because someone who feels 'not good enough' usually feels that way about everything.

Finding the cause and allowing the client to actually see the reality of that event, as in what the other person said wasn't necessarily the truth . . . *it was just an opinion* . . . can go a long way towards shifting the thought pattern. Forgiving that person for the hurtful comment is also key to finally releasing it.

I will often encourage the client to also build their own 'statue' of themselves looking confident, full of self-worth and self-esteem. I'll introduce the idea that they can actually look at themselves in a positive way from now on, and appreciate and acknowledge their own good qualities and ultimately feel proud about themselves.

Then I'll guide them through 'fading out' the scene that started their old mindset, to make it truly insignificant. This can then be followed with positive suggestion and repetition based around building self-confidence.

CHAPTER 18

WHERE'S MY 'WELL DONE'?

I've found that many clients through their early lives felt they received little or no acknowledgement. Whether it be lack of acknowledgement that they were important in the family unit, so that they were left feeling ignored or invisible, or whether they were aware there was no acknowledgement for something they'd achieved that they felt should have warranted a 'well done'. More specifically, praise from a parent or from someone who they were aware that what they thought, mattered.

This doesn't always mean that a parent continually ignored their child and never had a good word to say. Only that awareness was sparked off by possibly *only one* event when it wasn't forthcoming—and the client as a child was expecting it—it can then become a *focal point* for the client throughout their life. They start to focus on the 'lack of it', in fact, they seem to see that 'lack' everywhere, and this can develop into them feeling that it's vitally important for them to achieve that elusive praise.

This can result in them becoming high achievers, continually looking for ways to acquire that 'pat on the back'. Yet, when they do achieve their goal, they still never feel satisfied from having done so because they immediately move their focus on attaining their next goal and the all-important 'well done!' Alternatively, they can do the complete opposite, and carry around a feeling of 'what's the point?' They feel they are never appreciated even if they do something well, which results in procrastination, low self-esteem and under-achieving.

This is where people are so individual . . . and this illustrates beautifully how 10 people could all have the same issue, but that it can play out in each of their lives in completely different ways. This could be because of the *type* of event that sparked off the way of thinking differing from someone else's trigger, or because additional experiences have collectively given that person a unique way of looking at the world and their place in it.

One of the other interesting little nuances that I've noticed with this particular issue, is that if the client's parent they are wanting the praise from is elderly or ill at the time they come to see me, then on some level, they are aware that the opportunity to get that long-awaited acknowledgement is running out. When the realisation sets in that they might never get the 'well done' or 'I love you', the panic can set in and the anxiety can start. Consequently, this is often something I see in middle-aged clients who can't understand why they suddenly have an anxiety problem when they've never experienced it in their lives before.

But of course, the client isn't aware of this, and so they don't turn up at the office saying, 'I have anxiety because no one ever tells me they appreciate me and my dad is really ill and I think I'm getting worried I'll never hear those words.' It tends to be more like, 'I've started to get panic attacks recently and I don't know why—there seems to be no rhyme or reason to it, they just start suddenly and I don't know how to cope with them.'

Then comes the detective work to discover why they have that anxiety . . . so I start with my process of investigation to find their unique answers.

As we live in this world of being judged and compared, it is no wonder that we do seem to need praise to recognise that others value us in some way . . . especially our parents. They are the centre of our world for so many years and what they think matters—***big time!*** All the effort put into achieving something is well worth every second if the 'well done' is forthcoming. But, it can equally seem like total futility, even devastation, if it isn't.

If praise is virtually *never* given, then the child finds themself in a constant uphill struggle of trying to get even a flicker of recognition, and each time it doesn't come it's like another stab in the heart of rejection. This constant pursuit of praise can become a way of life, and although it's usually still directed at the parent, it can just as easily start to affect all areas of life, where winning praise for even the mundane things from just about anyone is sought after.

Using hypnosis, there are a few ways we can change this concept in the subconscious mind to allow it to let go of the fear that it won't ever get the one thing that it wants . . . for example, praise from a father. Again, the imagination is the key! I'll ask the client to picture themself standing face-to-face with their father and telling him of some of the things that they've achieved, so that they can see the pride on their father's face and hear him say the words, 'Well done Son, I'm so proud of you'.

This may seem strange because it's playing with the truth a little, but when you think about it, everybody achieves something in their life that does deserve praise. Often, if a parent doesn't give it where it's due, it's because of the parent's limitations within their personality that stop them from coming out with those words. In their heart, they would have known that it would be something that should be acknowledged.

I try to also instil a sense of the client being able to rely on themself for their 'pat on the back'. They know when they have achieved something worthwhile and all that should really matter is that they appreciate their own achievements and take the time to feel proud of themself. Again self-confidence, self-esteem and self-worth are all building blocks on which to work, and so I would include positive suggestion around adopting these attributes.

Carrying out these visualisations can bring peace back to the subconscious mind. It takes away the anxiety of the parent aging and possibly dying, as well as instilling a solid sense of self-esteem and self-worth in the client from which a sense of inner peace can evolve.

CHAPTER 19

REJECTION

Many issues, of course, overlap with others, and Rejection in particular overlaps with 'not belonging', not feeling good enough', 'no praise' and 'being judged'. However, the emphasis is more centred around a client's hyper-sensitivity to other people's rejection of them. Even if, in reality, it's quite a small rejection, it becomes something out of all proportion and can become magnified to the point of irrational jealous behaviour. Why? Because the 'rejectee' (no such word, but it serves a purpose so I'm using it) often sees the 'rejecter' as *choosing* someone or something else instead of them. This can escalate to the point that a person can see their spouse *choosing* to read a book instead of talking to them, as grounds for divorce!

As with any issue, the cause can be any number of things. There's the obvious rejection by a parent, whether it be a parent leaving the family and the child taking it personally, thinking that it must be their fault, or an everyday awareness of rejection that's compounded by the consistency of it, for example a parent never really wanting to spend any time with their child.

A parent leaving the family home can often result in the child feeling that they just aren't good enough or lovable enough for the parent to want to stay. While families split up for many different reasons, each child in that family will be focused on *their* part in the equation and often reflect it back on to themself, seeing themself as being to blame in some way.

The other thing I've found with seeing so many clients with this issue, is that when the clients are in hypnosis and regressed back to the memory of their family splitting up, the words that I hear many of them say are: 'I don't understand what's going on'. Of course, it's natural for parents to try to protect their children from the fall-out of a separation or divorce, and it's not always age-appropriate to discuss with the child the reasons for a separation, but it seems to be the *confusion* around the whole event that leaves children with the most issues they take into adulthood. Primarily because they come up with their own version of what went wrong, which I'm learning, is why more often than not, they seem to put *themselves* in the firing line.

The real problem with people who carry around the concept of 'people reject me' is that their happiness lies entirely in the hands of others. They can *only* feel good about themselves and their life if they feel important to another person, and the smallest sign of rejection can be magnified out of all proportion and seem like the end of the world. The strain this can put on a relationship is substantial, with their partner feeling stifled and confused, because often, they don't really understand what it is they've apparently done wrong.

Clients who come to me because they don't know how to curb their jealousy, are actually aware that they are behaving a little irrationally, and as a result, they try to hide or ignore their feelings. This though, just tends to make matters worse because the feelings that are getting suppressed, build up, until they come out in uncontrollable ways— very often anxiety symptoms or anger usually directed toward those closest to them.

For this reason, it's important to find out what happened in the client's life to make the subconscious mind become so focused on being rejected. It can simply be, one event that caused the subconscious' world to shift from being one where it knew its place in the family, and was always accepted as part of that family, to one where it realised that a parent could actually push them away, whether intentional or not.

Alternatively, this issue could come from a family environment where someone was *consistently* rejected by a parent, it then becomes almost a life-long struggle to gain that acknowledgement and reassurance that 'my dad does love me!' This is where the issue of having 'no praise' (previous chapter) becomes where the focus is for the client.

Again, once the cause has been located, we have to forgive the person who did the rejecting. I will often give the client a chance also to say to the 'rejecter' how it felt to be rejected. This gives the client the sense of 'I know I've been hurt, but I feel like I have had my say and I feel OK now'. This step is about finding a way to bring things back to a calm balance, and enabling the client to feel a sense of justice, where previously they felt unfairly treated . . . causing the subconscious to feel happy and safe again.

With Rejection, I often install the 'grey-scale', because it allows the introduction of other concepts into a relationship. That way, the subconscious mind doesn't just see that relationship as being black and white . . . as in, the client's spouse either accepts them *fully* and is happy to be with them 24 hours a day, or, if they're not willing to do that, then the client feels complete and *total* rejection. Currently, there's nothing in between these two extremes.

The 'grey-scale' introduces and asks the subconscious mind to accept lots of other possibilities into its awareness. It could be, for example, 'It's OK for my partner to spend time with other people.' This would enable the subconscious to not be fearful of that any longer, and to accept it as normal. Another shade of grey might be,

'It's OK for both me and my partner to have some 'me' time,' or 'It's OK when my partner chooses to work on his motorbike instead of being with me'. There's a myriad of other possibilities—other 'shades of grey'—that can be acceptable to the subconscious.

I might also ask the client to rehearse some of those new 'shades of grey' concepts, by imagining that they see their partner actually doing some of these things, while they themself notice that it feels OK and there's nothing to worry about.

As I also mentioned, clients with rejection issues tend to rely on their partners to make them happy, so it's also important to help them start developing their own internal happiness through building self-confidence, self-esteem and self-worth. Tuning into the 'self' helps them to reinforce that it's really good to have that 'me' time, so they can explore and find things that fulfil them, *regardless of what other people are doing.*

CHAPTER 20

CHILDHOOD RESPONSIBILITY OVERWHELM & HOW THE SUBCONSCIOUS SELECTS YOUR ANXIETY SYMPTOMS

This chapter expands on the previously mentioned aspect of how children adopt responsibility in their early years for what is going on in the family.

I've noticed whilst in regression, that people will often say things like: *'I was aware that Mum and Dad were arguing and that they could break up, so it occurred to me, that if I was really, really good, then that would cause less arguments and they'd stay together and everything would be alright.'*

I've found this sort of thing coming up time and time again . . . that a child witnessing the negative things going on within the family, whether it be between their parents or any other relatives, would take over the responsibility of the wellbeing of the family, by doing something in the hope of averting disaster. The problem being, that this level of responsibility is enormous for anyone, let alone a child. Ultimately, the action is also futile, because it's *impossible* to orchestrate everything and everyone within a family so that the household remains calm and balanced and everyone is happy—all the time.

Added to this, is the consequence of blaming of oneself when things inevitably go wrong!

Another slant on this issue, is when an older sibling assumes the protective role toward his or her younger brothers and sisters. Because when something happens to any of them, which, again, is inevitable at some stage, the overwhelming sense of blame for letting them down or being unable to protect them, can be all-consuming. It's no wonder it's easy to carry the concept of 'it's my fault' into adulthood.

When a client carries this perspective of themself around with them, it's important to placate the subconscious by assuring it that it isn't it's responsibility to take care of the whole world and everyone in it—and back in the childhood years, it *definitely was not* it's responsibility.

This can often be quite a hidden aspect of an issue, and it is amazing what it can attach itself to, which brings me to another interesting point . . . the subconscious can latch onto the most obscure and sometimes unrelated things in its manifestation of an issue. An aspect that adds to the sense of one's anxiety being *impossible* to decipher.

It has come to my notice, that when someone is triggering big emotions because of a specific event, (whether it happens at the cause or is re-sensitised later in life) the subconscious has an awareness of not *just* the focus of that event, but all sorts of other things that are going on around it at the same time. It can then pick any one, or a few of those things happening and make some seemingly strange and unrelated connections, which develop in a way that results in the client experiencing symptoms of anxiety. Remember, the subconscious isn't logical.

For example, a client who was the older sibling and was protective of his younger sister, found that the anxiety triggered from this awareness, latched onto having a needle at the dentist, resulting in a life-long issue of the 'fear of needles'.

This happened, because as the older sibling, he'd already experienced an injection and knew it hurt, and when his Mum took both him *and* his sister for the first time, he thought that his job as older brother was to protect his sister, but in this situation, he couldn't prevent her pain and so felt that he let her down. On that day, the emotional reaction sent alarm bells ringing, and the subconscious made a new connection, that of 'letting people down', and having an injection—simply because that was what was going on at the time.

Through finding this connection, he learned that his fear wasn't, and never had been, the pain of having an injection. His anxiety was about being unable to protect a loved one and feeling he'd let them down—it just so happened that when this awareness triggered for the first time, he was at the dentist and there were was a needle involved. Learning this ensured that we neutralised the *correct*, albeit less obvious part of the issue, and therefore the work was effective.

Another example is of a client who opposed a childhood 'love doesn't exist' belief system on his wedding day. On the day, he ate something that he reacted badly to and as a result during one of the car journeys, he thought that he would be sick. This sparked the subconscious to make a connection between its new awareness that a primary belief system was 'under attack' and the feeling of nausea that he suffered in the car. Soon afterwards, he started to feel sick *every time* he travelled in a car. Things got so bad that he started to avoid car journeys where possible which became a real problem in his day-to-day life. Again, the focus of his anxiety wasn't what appeared to be the fear of cars . . . it was the connection that the subconscious had made between feeling anxious that it's primary self-belief system was being challenged and the fact that it happened to be in the car feeling sick when this was happening.

This story just shows how delving and finding 'the cause' is essential. On the surface, most people would logically come to the conclusion that the wedding day was the start of this issue, but it went further back than that. It started in his childhood when his belief system was created that 'love doesn't exist' and so that is what we had to focus our work on, *not* just the car journey.

CHAPTER 21

FEAR OF FAILURE VS BEING A FAILURE

The awareness of failure is a fairly common belief-system that people adopt. It can intervene and disrupt people's lives in so many ways, whether it be not achieving life-long dreams and goals, or simply not getting all those odd jobs done around the house.

I've wondered to myself why this crops up so many times when working with clients, but, in essence, it comes back to that old coconut . . . 'being judged' . . . It's virtually impossible to get through our early lives without being aware that at some point, we didn't quite do as well as someone else.

The experience or experiences that cause the awareness of the potential to fail will obviously have a lot to do with how it's acted out and the intensity of its existence. For example, your awareness might be fairly minor if, when at school, one of your classmates who didn't really factor on your 'cool dudes' radar, just happened to mention that your painting wasn't very good. If nobody else heard the comment, then it wouldn't really upset you too much, and you'd probably just shrug it off and carry on painting. But, if the comment came from the teacher, in front of the whole class and all the kids in the class laughed at you, then your subconscious mind might make the connection that 'failing can open you up to ridicule and embarrassment', causing it to 'fear' failure. A reaction that in later life will probably have you not even starting things because the potential to fail is too scary to the subconscious mind . . . enter procrastination.

(Yes—I've used that classroom scenario yet again. The reason for this is that it shows you how just one stand-alone event can potentially have so many different outcomes and initiate different issues.)

However, the awareness of 'I _am_ a failure' is slightly different. If, for example, one of your dad's favourite sayings to you when you were younger was *'you're useless!'*, then you may find yourself making a bigger effort than most to try and achieve your goals in life. This could possibly even be as a way of sticking two fingers up to your dad! But despite this, you'll probably find yourself constantly self-sabotaging to ensure that all efforts definitely fail. Why? Because you believe yourself to *be* a failure and therefore you have to do whatever it takes to match that belief.

To help alleviate the heightened awareness of failure and after finding the cause, I might ask the client to imagine that the label of 'I'm a failure' be taken off and destroyed. Having got rid of it means it's no longer something they have to live up to. Then, of course, as I've taken something away, I would replace it with a better label such as one that says, 'I'm a success'.

I might also introduce the 'grey scale' to the subconscious mind to alleviate their anxiety about 'fearing failure'. The 'grey scale' would introduce the subconscious mind to the concept that it's okay to have a go at something and succeed, but it's equally okay to have a go at something and achieve somewhere between the extremes of *total* success and *total* failure. Since these two concepts are a long way apart and inflexible, we need to take the anxiety away from the pressure of having to fall into *just* these two categories.

Positive suggestion encouraging self-esteem and self-confidence is essential with this issue because these attributes can be virtually non-existent in someone who has had it drummed into them since early childhood that they're useless. As usual, these become the building blocks for introducing other positive attributes that the client has decided they would like.

CHAPTER 22

PERFECTIONISM

It's surprising how many people carry around the awareness of perfectionism . . . it's an interesting concept . . . it's like the 'fear of being judged' and the 'fear of failure' all rolled into one—*on steroids!*

There is often no rest for people who are perfectionists. It creeps into virtually every area of their life, and it's full of highs and lows, the extremes of *massive* satisfaction and *huge* disappointments. It can make them competitive, even over the little things. Oddly enough, I've had clients who panicked that if I helped them overcome their debilitating perfectionism, in turn, they would then be worried that their standards would drop. That would be *disastrous* . . . they'd hate to be someone who didn't do things right!

Now, I have to say, I've been known to be a bit of a perfectionist myself, and knowing how that affects me, it's truly a wonder that this book ever got started. The reason I say that, is because I've never written a book before. It's a tall order in my head, and if I can't do it perfectly, which is highly unlikely seeing as I've never done it before, then I shouldn't even start it.

I've had clients who have had this awareness *so* heightened in their minds that it literally freezes them with anxiety when they're carrying out even the littlest of things. The thought of not doing it perfectly is inconceivable, and so they'd rather not do it all. This is OK if it's something like painting a picture as it doesn't really make much of a difference whether you bring a picture into existence or not, but if it is something more crucial to living a normal life, like driving for example, then it can cause huge anxiety. If a perfectionist realises that they don't seem to have the co-ordination to be a good driver, then the thought of taking a test and possibly failing could be upsetting to the point of continually putting the whole thing off, even though they need to be able to drive in their everyday life.

Perfectionism can also make someone strive beyond normal reason to accomplish some goal they've set out for themselves, causing anxiety to kick in when something unexpected comes along to potentially jeopardise it. They can feel unsettled at the thought of something left unfinished, or not finished perfectly, and they can constantly go over and over in their minds what they did wrong. Then comes the inevitable and constant awareness that someone else would have seen the flaw—and, *'Oh my God, what would they be thinking?'*

Most people would just give up at some point, if something wasn't quite right . . . maybe shrug it off and put it down to experience. But perfectionists would most likely find themselves consumed by all these continual thoughts of beating themselves up, and that level of anxiety and fear, when it builds up, can simply stop them in their tracks.

I've found that childhood experiences connected with the onset of perfectionism are often entwined with a child's awareness of wanting to please a parent. Sometimes this can start from the child's need to be accepted and to belong by doing everything perfectly in a way that a parent would consider to be 'the right way'. Effectively, they are trying to live up to a parent's ideals, an aim which can be heightened if the parent is particularly worried about what other people think of them.

By regressing using hypnosis, once 'the cause' has been located and 'neutralised', then the subconscious can start to consider that not everything has to be done perfectly. It's OK just to 'have a go', just to enjoy the experience, and to just do it, without having to be better than anyone else. Once again, the 'grey scale' is ideal for introducing this new concept, for the client to allow all the other increments between success and failure into their awareness. They can then feel at ease with this concept, and not become anxious if their experience doesn't fall into either 'black or white'.

CHAPTER 23

OBSESSIVE COMPULSIVE DISORDER

Obsessive Compulsive Disorder (OCD) is usually all-encompassing and therefore disruptive in people's lives. They live a life where their choices seem to be taken away from them, they are slaves to their compulsions . . . but, paradoxically . . . even though they have seemingly no control over the things they are compelled to do, those actions make them feel they are in control of something.

Behind the compulsion is usually fear . . . fear that some disaster will occur if they don't carry out certain actions. Whether it be constantly cleaning to control the level of cleanliness in their environment for fear of germs, or they open and close a door six times before walking through it, because if they don't, they fear a catastrophe will befall someone they love, or they find themselves constantly repeating an action until they feel it has been done properly because they just fear not getting a physical movement exactly right.

OCD sufferers usually have a heightened awareness of their condition and understand that it's not at all logical, and that it may therefore be perceived by others as crazy. So, they will often try to hide it from those around them, again, for fear of judgement, which on top of everything else they feel they have to do, just adds to their level of anxiety. This can become all-consuming as well as exhausting mentally, and sometimes physically.

When working with clients living with OCD, whether the condition is fairly minor or more severe, as with all issues, the emotions behind the OCD are the key to finding the cause. Sufferers' heads are usually completely cluttered because of the unrelenting conversational battles taking place . . . what they feel compelled to do, trying to persuade themselves not to do it, justifying why they should, coming up with ways of trying to hide it. This continual inner turmoil, on top of the physical aspect of having to carry out certain tasks or movements, can all be *utterly* overwhelming—it seems that there is no rest or peace for them. Trying to wade through all of this to define the emotions behind their issue can, as you may expect, be a little more challenging than usual.

Even after finding and neutralising 'the cause', there's a lot of 're-training' for OCD sufferers. People's thoughts are *so* important . . . they are where *everything* starts, and those thoughts determine how they feel and then what they do.

A client with OCD has thoughts running rampant, of which they seem to have no control over. So part of the re-learning is to really rein in their galloping negative thoughts, encouraging them to recognise and acknowledge what they're thinking, but then switching them very quickly onto something more positive. Again, all clients are different, and after our work together, some clients may find that they just seem to start thinking and feeling differently in subtle ways that allow them to let go of the physical routines they'd been previously locked into. While with other clients the changes require more of a combination of both conscious and subconscious re-training, which is when I encourage clients to find active ways to think better thoughts more of the time. (For more on this, read the 're-programming' chapter). Amongst other things, it outlines practical techniques to interrupt negative thought processes.

CHAPTER 24

RELATIONSHIPS

When helping a client who has come to see me because they're having relationship issues, it can sometimes be more complicated because while there is more than one person involved in the troublesome relationship, often, only one person will come and see me. This can be because that person is unhappy and wants to find something to help themself feel happier, or, one person is unhappy and they persuade their partner to come and see me, so their partner can hopefully 'be fixed', which in turn will hopefully make them feel better because their partner has changed.

Even if both halves of a couple came to see me for help, I would see them individually and explain a few things up-front.

Firstly, that the work we'll do together is to make each person happy in their own right . . . for themselves . . . and not purely to conform to the other person's ideas of what their partner should be like.

Secondly, by the time people come for help, it's usually been quite some time after the issues have started . . . sometimes after years of unhappiness. This means that they have become fairly used to the way each person is, even though they've decided they don't like certain elements of the way the other person behaves. Also, as much as they want them to change, they may not change in quite the way the partner was hoping for. Therefore, even though they assume it's a change that would make their lives better, it may well bring new dynamics into the relationship which they might find difficult to adjust to. For example, if you're used to your partner never giving you compliments and not being attentive towards you—how would you feel if suddenly they had a complete about-turn and were proclaiming their undying love every five minutes. Okay, it's a bit of an exaggeration I know—but you get the point! You may assume you'd love it, but part of you wouldn't know how to respond and it might even get on your nerves—who knows?

And thirdly, I discuss with clients how each person's idea of improvement and happiness is different. The work we do together is based on helping each individual be happy within themself, but there's no guarantee it will help the 'relationship', even if it does make the individual happier. One of a couple might find themself making many positive changes, leading them to realise that being with their current partner is not good for them and that parting company may actually be the only way for them to feel happier.

I have also had clients who've asked me to effectively 'erase' all memories of their 'ex'. It may be because it has become too painful for them to think about them now they've parted, or maybe they've been obsessing over them and can't stop the thoughts . . . Either way, I never agree to this—ever! There are a few different reasons for this:

Firstly, effectively erasing 'someone' doesn't mean erasing *just* the memory of them in isolation . . . it would mean erasing the surrounding events attached to their memory. Huge chunks of experiences could be erased, everything you experienced that they were involved in. Can you imagine trying to cope with that? It would be a *complete* nightmare for you to try and make sense of things. It would cause utter chaos . . . especially if it had been a long relationship.

Secondly, I believe that people are in our lives for us to learn from our experiences with them. If you take all of that away, what have you learned? Surely, it would be more beneficial to see why they were having such a difficult time letting them go. What are the underlying insecurities? What have they learnt about their time together and why they parted? This is what's going to help them more than anything—not erasing massive chunks of their life.

CHAPTER 25

PHYSICAL PAIN

I have noticed that when an experience I regress clients back to involved some physical pain, the physical pain seems to act as an amplifier to the event, making something that wouldn't have been dominant in their life's experiences into something that is prominent.

For example, if we take a typical classroom scenario of the teacher berating a pupil in front of the whole class for failing an assignment, that is one level of awareness . . . possibly 'fear of failure'. However, if during the incident, the berated pupil also happened to fall off his chair and bang his head, and the other kids all laughed, then that bit of physical pain could magnify the whole experience.

Again, this is just an observation of mine, but it seems to be a consistent one which is why I have mentioned it. We know, of course, that emotions are triggered by the subconscious mind and it's the emotional experiences and consequent automatic reactions that cause many of our issues as human beings. However, as quantum physics is starting to prove, the mind and body is more 'connected' than we thought, and in fact, it's the mind where physical disease and illnesses start.

So, in light of this, it's no wonder that the subconscious mind would factor physical pain into the grand scheme of things, and use it to amplify an emotion.

I personally haven't worked extensively with clients with physical issues like disease, or illness or pain management, but I have had clients who, whilst having an internal emotional shift, have also, had physical changes take place. For example, I had a client who came to me for anxiety, stress and relationship issues and after 'week two' of working together, she said, 'I don't know what's happened, but I don't seem to need to wear my glasses anymore.' Another client came to me for an anxiety issue and after her first session, all her dermatitis cleared up virtually over-night.

With both of these clients, I wasn't aware of their physical issues and so had given absolutely no suggestions regarding those issues. It's my understanding though, that the subconscious had created those physical symptoms within the body as a result of the underlying emotional issue, and as we worked on the underlying emotional issue, it then cleared up everything that was involved with it, including the physical symptoms.

It seems to me that the subconscious mind initiates physical pain and disease for a reason . . . it's never there 'just because'. It serves some sort of purpose whether it's an outlet of negative feelings that affect the body's cells, or whether it's in the form of self-sabotage for a weight management client whose self-belief system says they need their weight for protection. The subconscious steps in with 'injury' to a joint or muscle to stop further exercise, therefore preventing weight loss and maintaining protection.

Science is proving this mind-body connection more and more, and so when you combine this knowledge with how hypnosis works, I'm sure you can see the potential for all kinds of wonderful changes . . . not just emotional ones. I'm sure you can see that hypnotherapy has the potential to help with many different physical ailments and symptoms. There are hypnotherapists who specialise in this area who have fantastic results with the physical aspects of people's issues. Indeed you may also be aware that some medical surgeons have and do use hypnosis instead of anaesthetic for pain-free surgery.

> *Who knows how modern medicine will progress as it further accepts this aspect of the mind. It seems we may all have the ability within us to heal ourselves.*

CHAPTER 26

INFERTILITY

By the time I see female clients for fertility issues, they are usually at the stage of having had several failed IVF attempts, and the reality of having their own child feels like it's slipping away . . . a situation that adds to their over-all anxiety.

Added to this stressful situation, is the physical and financial stresses of ongoing fertility treatment. Added together, it doesn't make for the calm and relaxed body-mind state that's needed for successful implantation and hosting of the embryo.

I've not worked extensively with fertility clients, but some things have definitely jumped out as being an integral part of their issue. The main one being that the subconscious has an awareness that the world isn't a safe place to be, and more specifically the woman usually feels that on some level she will be unable to protect her child from these probable dangers.

The subconscious could arrive at this conclusion because of the client's own childhood experience of having felt completely unprotected, vulnerable and unsafe. It knows the fear of being hurt is justified and the thought of their *own* child going through something as painful is absolutely *unthinkable!* Or maybe, a past experience has shifted the focus more on the client *herself,* maybe she feels incapable of protecting other people and as a result she wouldn't be able to trust herself to to keep her own child safe.

I've mentioned this aspect of 'protecting others' and 'letting people down' before in relation to older siblings of a family. Indeed there may well be some correlation here too—I've noticed a high percentage of the infertility clients I've worked with have been the older sibling. Maybe this is because the older sibling is given a huge responsibility of protecting others at a time in their lives when they are most ill-equipped to do so, both mentally, emotionally and physically. Therefore they are more likely to get it wrong and when they do, they're more likely to blame themselves.

I am not indicating that *all* infertility issues are caused by the 'fail to protect' or that the 'failure to protect' *always* causes infertility. I just feel that there is a connection that's worth noting.

The most important aspect when working with a client who feels that the world is so perilous, is to help them to firstly feel safe, and then to encourage them to be able to trust themself to have all the abilities required to protect a child of their own. The subconscious is looking at the world with childlike eyes, after all, most of what it holds as 'the way the world works' was shown to it through childhood. Therefore in our sessions, I ask the subconscious to acknowledge that since the childhood experience that caused the issue, the client has matured and learned through many other life experiences, and so, focus on this new knowledge that would allow them to care for a child and to keep it safe. Instilling the fact that indeed they can fully trust themself to love and protect a child of their own.

The other aspect to focus on, is the combining of these feelings. If the subconscious feels the world is dangerous, and the client is unable to protect their child, that effectively proves to it that the potential loss of a child is highly probable, and is thus too painful a thing to consider enduring. This causes the subconscious to use its ultimate powers of protection to keep the client from experiencing unimaginable emotional distress at the loss of a child by not letting it have the child in the first place. The client may well be suffering greatly from being unable to have a child of their own, but the subconscious' fear of loss is far greater and therefore wins the battle!

When trying to calm the subconscious about the potential loss of a child, I am careful not to be unrealistic. I cannot say to it that the child would *never* be harmed in any way, or *never* fall ill or even pass away. If I got the subconscious mind to accept that concept, then if one of those things occurred (and we know all children become ill at some stage), then the subconscious could enter a severe state of panic when it did happen.

Instead I talk to it about life in general . . . with a slight grey-scale aspect. As in, a child is here to experience all manner of things—the good, the bad, the ups and the downs. These are all perfectly natural. Yes, it's the parents' job to guide and protect *where possible*, but more importantly it's *alongside* their child, so that child can learn and experience life with all its many shades of grey as it's supposed to. I feel this perspective calms the subconscious mind and appeals to it to re-evaluate the unrealistic concept that all children must be 100% happy/safe/protected/healthy all the time, and accept that there are many increments of life that are a natural part of the human experience also.

But, whatever the cause and reason behind a client's infertility, the subconscious, I believe, has affected the physical body up to this point, so that pregnancy is unlikely. Some clients see their infertility as their body rejecting the embryo, others perceive it as the embryo not wanting to stay because the environment isn't healthy or welcoming. For this reason, it's important to understand how the client sees her own body and why it's not allowing the pregnancy, so that we can re-frame the old thought pattern to something positive.

I believe that the body has a natural state of well-being, but that it's our thoughts and issues that become the blocks that stop the natural flow of that well-being, which in turn causes *any* medical condition. To overcome this, I might ask the client therefore to imagine those blocks finally being taken away. To imagine a healthy uninterrupted flow finally going through the body, specifically re-aligning the reproductive organs to do whatever they have to do to become a place that is warm, welcoming and safe for the embryo, as well as somewhere the embryo would *want* to be.

Projecting forward and allowing the client to daydream about *finally* holding their baby in their arms is also powerful, as by now they might have stopped allowing themselves to dream in such a way because the emotions of an unsuccessful implantation would be even more devastating for them. This mindset in itself becomes a huge part of the problem since their negative thought processes become the *biggest* blocks preventing any success.

As with all issues, I use the same process of finding the cause . . . asking the subconscious why it won't allow the client to have a child . . . then neutralising the cause. Then I follow up with lots of positive suggestions to allow the physical body, as well as the mind, to start adapting to thoughts of welcoming a child.

CHAPTER 27

CHILDHOOD
SEXUAL ABUSE

I t's becoming apparent in modern society just how rife sexual abuse is . . . that's not to say it's necessarily more common in modern society, only that it's more talked about than it used to be, so it's only now that we're really seeing the extent of the problem.

I too have been at the hands of a sexual abuser as a teenager and so it is with some experience that I can talk about this particular issue, but what I write is also a general culmination of observations I've noted through seeing many clients who have experienced sexual abuse. The main thing I discovered when my particular experience was finally brought out into the open, was that as I started to actually talk to my friends about it, I became horribly aware of how many other people had undergone a similar experience. I could hardly believe it, and at first, it gave me a horrible feeling of instability and vulnerability . . . not so much for me, but for the children of today and tomorrow. I suddenly felt it was happening everywhere, there was no control over the situation, and that young children everywhere were at risk. At that moment I just wanted to go out and save the world from it all.

There's been many a client, that when I've asked them at the end of the information gathering part of the process, if there was anything else relevant that they hadn't talked about when answering my questions, has answered, 'Well, yes, I suppose I should mention that I was sexually abused as a child.'

When you read this book and see how the mind works and how it forms us as people, then I guess we also have to ask the question, 'What happened in society to create so many abusers?' I don't know the answer to this question as I haven't had any self-confessed sexual 'offender' clients . . . only their victims. One of the things I've noticed in collecting information about sexual abuse, is that many of the abusers are children themselves . . . the victim's older teenage brother, or friends of their siblings, or cousins.

Sexual abuse comes in many forms and, not to belittle any one experience of it, it also comes in varying degrees of seriousness. But, at the end of the day, whether the abuse is minor (which in my head is where I'd place mine) or major, the victim is usually left confused. This confusion is a mixture of different elements all rolled into one.

These are the sorts of things victims find themselves asking, sometimes at the time of the abuse, and sometimes years later . . .

What Just Happened?

Depending on the age of the victim at the time of the abuse, depends on how confusing this part of the equation is. I've seen clients who have suffered abuse as young as two years old . . . at that age there's a great deal of *'what was that?'* Yet, even at such a young age and having no conscious awareness of the sexual act, they still seem to have an awareness, that something was *definitely* not right— and that it was *definitely not* supposed to happen!

Indeed, no matter what age the abuse occurs, confusion seems to be overwhelming. Trying to 'compute' all the aspects of the event, both physically and mentally, is almost impossible . . . especially, as underlying nearly all sexual abuse is the pressure the victim experiences trying to figure out what to do about it. Important factors in that decision are the age of both the victim and the abuser, whether the abuser is known to the victim or not, whether any threats have been made, and whether the abuse is a one-off event or on-going.

How Could A Person I Trusted Do That To Me?

If the abuser is a family member or trusted family friend, then from a subconscious' point of view, this is earth shattering! Up to that point in time, there was a sense of safety in the fact that there were certain people that could <u>always</u> be relied upon and trusted. This is one of those 'this is the way the world works' belief systems that keep a person's levels of security nice and balanced—so when that belief is profoundly abused, the subconscious goes into a massive spin and panic. It suddenly wakes up to the horrible truth that 'people can hurt me' . . . even those that it thought it could always count on to keep it safe.

This level of 'broken-trust awareness' can also extend to others around them at the time . . . for example, someone might find themselves thinking 'why didn't my mum stop this from happening to me?' If they did actually go on to tell their mum, but she didn't believe them and therefore didn't do anything about it . . . then the subconscious' sense of vulnerability extends even further. This can cause a belief of, 'there really is *no one* in this world who can protect me from bad things happening.'

As you've become aware by now, the subconscious likes to feel safe, and this is about as 'unsafe' as it can get.

Was It My Fault?

Even if the abuser doesn't persuade the victim it's their fault—maybe as a threat to keep their silence—the victim can still question their own part in the equation. They can often find themselves coming up with all sorts of ways to blame themselves for what happened. Together with the confusion of trying to sort through one's feelings, is the element that I've heard some clients reveal to me, that at some level, they liked the attention. This is especially prevalent with ongoing abuse usually occurring in the teenage years by someone older whom they know. Although they knew they didn't like the actual physical aspect of the abuse, a part of them did like the feeling that they were the centre of someone's attention and that this person seemingly 'loved' them enough to be so totally focused on them.

Of course, through the teen years is when we tend to have our 'where do I belong?' wobble anyway. Receiving such intense attention from another person, albeit unwanted and frightening, can leave the teenage victim going through a myriad of conflicting emotions, including massive waves of guilt as they struggle with these confusing feelings. These feelings can be immense, to the point of overwhelm, and so the victim will do all they can to shut them down.

What Should I Do? Who Should I Tell?

This is where the enormity of what has happened can become even more of a horrible, confusing mess in the mind of the victim. They feel that they either want to or should tell someone, but all the possible scenarios of what could happen if they did, can become all-encompassing as they go round and round in their head. I know in my case, I chose not to tell anyone because I was worried that other people in the family would be hurt by the news and that it could cause divorce, splitting of the family and so on. I just couldn't bring myself to do it . . . little did I know I wasn't the only victim . . . and other members of my family were carrying around exactly the same worries in their own heads and as a result also said nothing. The true details only came out years later when I was talking to one such family member and must have said something that alluded to what happened. In that moment we both looked at each other and said, 'My God . . . it happened to you too?'

Then, of course, we started to realise that other people could be at risk, and now as adults, we saw the necessity of something needing to be done. That's when the guilt set in because we worried that others had been affected and we could have stopped it if we'd said something earlier. Of course, at the time and being young, none of us had the ability, the bravery, or the confidence to make those kinds of decisions. Instead, for me, as a child, I simply accepted it as 'just one of those things', and something I tried to avoid thinking about as much as possible—including trying to avoid the question of 'What to do?'

So generally, whether the victim thinks it best not to tell anyone, or they tell someone and they are not believed, the sense of vulnerability for that child can be overwhelming. Their whole world as they have known it up to that point, has come crumbling down—and the subconscious is confused, not knowing what's going on, suddenly everything is different and potentially dangerous, and the subconscious mind doesn't like that one bit! But, it has to find a way to move on, so it goes into survival mode and protects as much as possible.

It has amazed me how the subconscious somehow incorporates this new, awful reality and carries on. I've listened to some clients talk so matter-of-factly about their experience, especially when the abuse has become 'just a part of their life', because the abuse has been ongoing, over years and years. As sad as it is, the subconscious survival instinct really is amazing.

How Can I Get Over This?

Helping someone move on from sexual abuse can be a challenge, because applying my process means ultimately asking the client to forgive someone for one of the worst things one human being can do to another; that of showing the victim that nothing is safe and that someone can 'invade' them at any time and they are completely powerless to stop or change anything.

One of the first things I'll ask the client to do is to imagine their abuser is there with them and they can say exactly what they want to them. This way, their abuser understands exactly what they did and what effect it has had on them. People may shout, swear and cry during this section which can be therapeutic in itself . . . to finally 'have a voice' and to be heard, gives them back some power.

As hard as the forgiveness part is, it's also the most profound; the weight lifted off their shoulders can be immense. The other difficult aspect of doing this is that the client feels that the abuser is getting away with something they shouldn't be able to. I try to help clients see this as more of a 'letting go' than a 'letting them off the hook', because this is ultimately for the client's own good, so they don't have to continue dragging the memories and emotions around with them in a way that has caused such a negative effect on their life.

'Fading out' the memory in the subconscious is also an essential part of the 'neutralising', it ensures the subconscious isn't using it as a constant, fundamental trigger that's contributing to their anxiety symptoms. Again, we're not saying it didn't ever happen, we're just re-framing it and re-filing it so that the client can make way for new and better ways of thinking, feeling and doing.

CHAPTER 28

COPING WITH DEATH

D eath is a natural part of life, but one we always seem to be so ill-equipped to cope with. I've had clients come to me because of anxiety over coping with the death of loved-ones, and I've also had clients come to me to help them cope with their own impending death due to diagnosis of an incurable disease.

It's natural, as well as essential, to feel and express the emotions that death and dying evoke in a person . . . but often, clients are brought up with a mind-set of *not* showing the emotions, especially the negative ones . . . like grief and pain or expressing these through crying. The first thing that usually happens when a child cries, is that an adult immediately rushes over to find out what's wrong, and then quickly encourages the child to '*stop* crying'. So from an early age, children are actively encouraged to stifle and cut off their emotions that should really be felt, expressed and then let go of. Interestingly, stopping a child from crying is probably more about the adult's wish to make themselves feel better, because maybe it makes them feel uncomfortable in some way, perhaps the noise is upsetting or they can't stand the thought of their child being in pain. To stop someone crying = stopping the pain.

Clients who have struggled to cope with the loss of a loved one, often come to me for all sorts of 'surface' reasons that effectively hide the cause . . . but after digging down and finding 'the cause', we find that it was the passing of a loved one that has been at the base of their anxiety. The loss of family and friends creates that change in a person's life of not knowing what will happen next as a result of that death, and as you're now aware, 'change' and the 'unknown' is an uncomfortable place for the subconscious to be.

Unresolved grief can be channelled in all sorts of ways. I've had clients that developed OCD traits . . . they started off by collecting things that they'd associated with their dead relative, as a way of keeping them close. Only then their obsessive need to collect and hoard became the focus and such an overwhelming part of their every-day life that it ended up disguising the reason behind it.

I've had a client who allowed his suppressed feelings of grief to affect his marital relationship. His grief was so intense at the disbelief of losing his parents before he got married, that when he did marry, he struggled to not 'blame' his wife for being lucky enough to still have her parents, when he couldn't have his. It seemed such an unfair situation to him that he started to resent her for it. He didn't consciously understand his feelings, but the subconscious let him become aware of it when we did his regression . . . it always knows the answers!

If someone can't find a way to process their grief, I've found that they can end up not allowing themselves to remember their loved one in any positive way. Why? Because the pain of their loss becomes *so* massive that they endeavour to cut off *all* memories and put up an immediate barrier at the slightest thought of their loved one popping into their mind. It often progresses in a way that their loved one's memories become tainted and are seen as upsetting and negative, which is an awful shame.

To help overcome this, I help the client re-frame what has become a negative connection to memories of their loved one in their mind . . . so they acknowledge that, in fact, everything that ever happens to them becomes a memory almost immediately, and that they can *choose* the ones that they would like to focus and reflect on, ideally those that would give them loving, positive feelings. They can then *choose* to enjoy these memories in the future, rather than running away from them. Yes, they may cry at first when they finally allow themselves to stop suppressing and then reconnect with those memories, but the crying will pass as will the fear and sadness. Slowly they will start to feel better as they tune into a positive memory . . .

> *. . . again this is centred around my belief that it's best to 'feel', acknowledge and then let the bad feelings subside, so that they can be replaced by better ones—rather than avoiding, suppressing and hiding from them.*

I would ask clients, whilst in hypnosis, to focus on a positive memory and to make it truly big and vibrant, then recollect how they felt at the time . . . to actually re 'feel' it now. This takes all the negativity and fear out of remembering a loved one who has passed, allowing the client to focus instead on what they loved about that person and the happy times they shared with them. Essentially, it's 're-planting' positive feelings and specifically connecting those feelings to the image of their loved one, so that in the future they can enjoy reminiscing happily.

CHAPTER 29

WEIGHT MANAGEMENT & SMOKING

'*Why have you grouped these two together?*' I here you ask. 'Surely these are two of the biggest issues that a hypnotherapist will see . . . I'm surprised you haven't written a whole book on each one of these!'

The reason I have done so, is that in my view:

> *Eating too much (or too little) and smoking aren't*
> *really 'the' issues . . . they are simply the symptoms*
> *of any one of the other issues in this book.*

When you over-eat consistently, and/or continually crave unhealthy food, then you're not eating for the sake of the food itself, you're eating whenever you feel you're not good enough in some way. You're eating because you fear rejection. After all, if you don't attract a partner because you're overweight, then you won't be rejected by them . . . you're eating because being overweight is a fantastic way to maintain your self-belief system that you're a failure—you can't even eat right!

Remember that I said the subconscious will often attach any number of things that are going on at the same time an issue starts? Eating is something we do many times a day, so is therefore likely to be at the top of the list of possible things the subconscious can choose from to connect to an issue . . . purely because we do it a lot and it's readily available.

Food is also one of the first comforters we get in life . . . just after birth, we cry and feel uncomfortable, along comes some warm milk and a big cuddle to make everything feel immediately better. You can imagine, therefore, the subconscious makes the connection: 'food = feel better'. We eat for comfort, we eat for a false sense of security, we might also eat so that people will continue to reject us because we're too over-weight . . . and we eat because of the underlying issue that the subconscious has attached to food.

Smoking itself isn't 'the' issue . . . like eating, you smoke for different reasons. Maybe at first it was to gain your sense of belonging to your peers by joining in with them, or for fear of being rejected if you didn't. After all, why would you do something that was so bad for you? Maybe, because to the subconscious mind, the fear of being rejected was *far* greater than the fear of experiencing breathing in foul-tasting smoke and coughing your lungs up.

The subconscious could also have made an 'illogical' connection that smoking actually seems to be quite good for you—because, as you strive to overcome the initial shock of having to inhale smoke, it recognises that it seems to have had a calming effect on you by relieving some of the anxiety you felt about 'not being good enough'. It's become aware that your peers have indeed accepted you as part of their group. So, as far as it's concerned, tobacco is fantastic stuff, therefore it assists you to keep doing it . . . remember, it always does things that it thinks are for your benefit.

Then there's the whole 'habit thing'. The subconscious learns by repetition . . . how many times a day do you put your hand to your mouth to take a puff on a cigarette? The action just becomes <u>so</u>

ingrained that many smokers are half way through a cigarette before they're consciously acknowledging that they're even doing so.

So for me, I'm more interested in the underlying issue and the cause of smoking and eating disorders, because when you find that and neutralise it, then the symptoms of smoking and eating the wrong way can be let go of by the subconscious, and it's more likely to adopt the new positive reprogramming.

CHAPTER 30

NOW WHAT?

There are so many other issues I could write about, but then this book could end up being ten volumes long! I have included the ones that I've come across the most . . . the ones that have really stood out as being common aspects of human behaviour—but also I've included things that I've found to be interesting and/or surprising.

As you've been reading this book, you may have identified with much of the content, because we probably all have a bit of most things within us—just at different levels to everyone else . . . our own special mixed bag of 'stuff'.

I've not written about any one issue in its entirety, there are, I'm sure, many more complex aspects, psychologically-speaking, to *all* of the issues I've mentioned . . . but that is not what this book is about.

The aim has been to keep this book as concise, basic and as simple as possible . . . as indeed is my therapy. It's effectiveness lies in its simplicity. ***Everyone already has all of their own answers*** locked away in the subconscious mind . . . and all it takes is for a hypnotherapist to help unlock them.

So, to answer the question, *'Now what?'* . . .

As I mentioned at the beginning of this book . . . I can hardly believe that this wonderful, effective and relatively quick and easy tool is not more widely used. I know first-hand how it has helped *so* many people overcome their anxiety—so if this is true, why don't more people know about this? Why isn't everyone doing it? Why haven't *you* already done it? The answer is—**FEAR!**

Fear of the unknown, fear of your own emotions, fear of hypnosis, *fear of fear!* It's the biggest thing holding us all back, and it's at the core of our anxiety. Don't you find it interesting that the very thing standing in the way of us overcoming our fear is our fear? It's my deepest wish that this book goes a long way to eliminating the 'fear' aspect of what's holding anyone back from getting the help that they need—using Hypnotherapy.

I would urge YOU, if you've been living with *any* form of anxiety to go and find a qualified hypnotherapist to help make those changes that you've only dreamed about, but probably thought were impossible. Find YOUR own answers, get to know who you *really* are, and gain a greater understanding of yourself in a wonderfully positive way, so as to contribute to your own self-development. **_You don't have to live with anxiety_** . . . there _is_ indeed an answer. There _is_ a way to move forward and find your inner peace—whatever that means to you. Use this knowledge to start to live the life that you want . . . *anxiety free!*

Hypnotherapy is not as widely-used as it could be—if it was more accepted, more people would consider using it, more people would find the help they need, whether it be for physical and/or emotional issues. I really hope this book contributes in some way to bringing hypnotherapy into people's awareness, so it can be considered as more of an 'everyday' therapy, rather than just for 'open-minded' people. Maybe it can be studied, understood and enhanced, even more than it currently is, because this all goes towards helping more people everywhere.

AFTERWORD

I first met Alexandra Hopkins 2 years ago when we began working alongside each other. A friendship soon developed, as well as a solid professional relationship. Although we both work independently of each other with most of our clients, at times we found that working together and combining psychology and hypnotherapy with clients who are having particular difficulty, would be even more effective. Our unique therapeutic approach has bought many successes. We have a similar attitude to mind health, we work well together and clients love the supporting relationship we offer. They feel safe; many for the first time.

Hypnotherapy in itself, in my opinion, is a valid form of therapeutic intervention—so much so, that I have been through this process with Alexandra myself, as the client. I experienced first-hand that when it is used skillfully, it can be another important modality in the therapeutic process to understand and care for the self. In my particular situation, hypnotherapy helped me to hear my inner voice in a different way and identify an unhealthy dialogue my subconscious was having to my conscious mind. I was stuck in sabotage, fearful of letting go of the fear of judgement and criticism. I reacted to certain situations where I felt an injustice; I withdrew and froze with self-doubt. *I'm not good enough.* After working through this with Alexandra in hypnotherapy, we managed to remove the final part of this sabotage and replace it with a healthier framework. Now here I am writing this article for the world to see . . . woohoo!

With a skilled practitioner, as is the case with Alexandra, hypnotherapy is a safe option. You, the client, manage the process and pace while the hypnotherapist takes care of the exploration and meaning into your unique set of sabotages, triggers and behaviours. Together, you work on a manageable conclusion.

As I read through this book, I was heartened by the intricacy and depth of knowledge Alexandra brings to the reader in an easy to understand format. I encourage you to read this book. Whether you are a practitioner or someone who wants to understand the wonders of hypnotherapy and how it can help you, this book will benefit you to appreciate the workings of the mind and the important role the subconscious has in affecting the way we think and feel. You can then make up your own mind as to what to do for yourself with the information you will have once completing this outstanding book. The choice is yours . . .

Enjoy reading this wonderful manuscript, as I did. A fantastic account of the role of the subconscious in all of its' glory. Great work Alexandra! I knew you could do it!

And to you, the reader, from my heart to yours . . . may happiness find you everywhere ☺

Jennifer Wilson, Bachelor of Psychology,
Nationally Registered Psychologist, Associate
Member of the Australian Psychological Society.

For more information on Jennifer Wilson, please go to:

www.lifeskills.com.au or contact Jennifer on
email jennifer.wilson@lifeskills.com.au

ABOUT THE AUTHOR

Alexandra Hopkins was born in the UK and moved to live permanently in Western Australia at the age of 22 years old, where she married and had two sons.

Her working life, for many years, revolved around the family Interior Design business, with her passion for hypnotherapy being ignited later on in life. With a huge change in circumstances, with the end of her 20 year marriage, it was time for a new direction and focus.

After qualifying as a hypnotherapist, she opened her own clinic in Joondalup, Western Australia, where her experience of working with hundreds of clients as a Clinical Hypnotherapist has culminated in the writing of this book. The more that she witnessed amazing results, time and time again, the more she felt the need to share this information with as many people as possible. Her aim is to wake the world up to the effectiveness of this wonderful, quick and easy 'tool of change', so more and more people can benefit from it.

Alexandra finds herself constantly amazed each and every day at the results her clients have experienced, and is both humbled and proud to be part of that experience . . .

'There is nothing more rewarding in life then being part of the process of someone finding their own happiness'.

Alexandra Hopkins,
Clinical Hypnotherapist